PORTRAIT OF THE ISLE OF WIGHT

Portrait of the
ISLE OF WIGHT

by

LAWRENCE WILSON

ROBERT HALE · LONDON

© *Lawrence Wilson 1965 and 1972*
First published July 1965
Reprinted February 1966
Second edition October 1972
Reprinted 1975

Robert Hale & Company
63 Old Brompton Road
London S.W.7

ISBN 0 7091 3319 7

Printed and bound in Great Britain by
REDWOOD BURN LIMITED
Trowbridge & Esher

To RUPERT

who barked and romped on the island downs

Acknowledgements

To the late Mr. F. S. Green, County Librarian, my sincere thanks are due for helping me to select and consult in comfort the most useful items from the mass of literature contained in the Isle of Wight room at the County Seely Library in Newport. For their assistance in various ways I should also like to thank Miss Geer of Freshwater, Mr. J. D. Jones, Curator of the Carisbrooke Castle Museum, the former County Planning Officer, Mr. R. W. Rose, and Dr. J. B. Williamson of Ventnor. I am also indebted for written advice to Mr. L. H. Baines, Clerk of the County Council, and the County Archivist, Mr. E. G. Earl; and, for their assistance in supplying material for the second edition, to Mr. Packwood and Mr. Cadman of the County Planning Office and to Mr. Brenchley of the Isle of Wight Tourist Board. Above all, I am very grateful to my wife, an ardent lover of the island, for her suggestions and encouragement during the writing of this book.

Contents

Illustrations

ACKNOWLEDGEMENTS

The photographs in this book are reproduced by permission of the following: Mr. W. L. C. Baker, nos. 1, 14 (*top*), 19, 20; Messrs. Beken of Cowes, 23, 24; Mr. Robin Fletcher, 3, 6, 8, 9 (*bottom*), 10, 16; Mr. Harold Hayles, 2, 4; Mr. H. K. Merwood, 5, 7, 9 (*top*), 11; Messrs. W. J. Nigh & Sons Ltd., 13, 14 (*bottom*); Mr. P. P. Mason, 21; the Mansell Collection, 15 (*bottom*); Roy J. Westlake, 17, 18, 22; Mrs. L. Wilson, 12.

I

THE ROUND TRIP

"I LIKE this island," said the man in the hotel, gazing out over the lawn fringed with oak trees that sloped down towards Freshwater Bay. "You can really get away from the rat-race. Do you know, I walked five miles over the downs this afternoon and only saw three people!"

"Yes," I replied. "It's very empty just now. The season doesn't start until next month, in April."

"And meanwhile they say that every man-jack in this island has got practically an acre to himself. Phew! . . . Makes you think!"

"It's extraordinary, isn't it, the contrast between the island now and at the peak of the season? It's like an empty garden at the moment, but just you see it in July or August!"

"I have," he said. "I used to come year after year with my family. We stood for two hours once, waiting to get off Ryde Pier. That was August Bank Holiday. Still, it was worth it. In season or out of season, the island's always the same. They have got freedom here. It's something to do with the sea, I think, lapping all round you. And the downs —those views. They are always different, depending on the weather and the time of day. To me the whole place is alive—with gulls, waves, clouds, breezes. Do you know what I mean?"

"Yes, I do. It's a life that goes on quite independently of the people. I was in church last Sunday, that little thatched church by the bay. A window was open and there was sunshine and green fields outside. With due respect to him, I couldn't listen to the parson—that other life was so much more potent."

"Yes, it's strong," said the man, an oldish man, with sudden emphasis. "It kind of calls you."

"Tennyson felt the same."

"Ah! Tennyson! But I'm not a poet. All I know is, I find something I need in this island. . . ."

There was a pause, then the old man said quietly: "I shall come to retire in this place."

We looked at the fields gently sloping to a V with a small triangle of sea beyond—the selfsame view that persuaded Tennyson over a hundred years ago to make his home in Freshwater. From behind us the low sun was shining on the bare branches of the trees. I thought of the catchwords applied to the Isle of Wight—"The Garden Isle", "England in miniature"—of the statistics—23 miles by 13, 148 square miles, 60 miles of coast—and of the enthusiasm with which local people had urged me to climb this down, explore that chine. After doing all this, reading many books and exploring the island, I felt it was essential, amid the mass of detail and the great variety of the scenery, to start this book with a single overall impression. But what should it be? I felt that I could do no better than quote that conversation with the old man and his phrase: "They have got freedom here."

The first aspect of this freedom, apart from the scenery, is negative, admittedly, but very important. There are no trunk-roads on the island, no diesel trains surging through the valleys, no biscuit-box skyscrapers, no conspicuous slums, few factories and those confined to certain areas, and no reckless spread of bungalow suburbia. Never, throughout the length and breadth of the Wight, have I experienced that sickening shock to the senses provoked so often on the mainland by some terrible monstrosity ruining a lovely stretch of countryside or by endless ribbon development. Here the towns—Newport, East and West Cowes, Ryde, Sandown/Shanklin and Ventnor—are narrowly circumscribed. You go into them and come out of them, and there's an end to it. Immediately outside these towns you are back again amid rolling hills and plains, with curious old villages, delightful glimpses of the sea, stretches of nodding wild flowers—unspoilt, ever-changing countryside.

For six months in the year, in the off-season, the inhabitants are free, too, from the sense of haste that prevails on the mainland. Forty per cent of them are engaged in the tourist trade and from October to April many of them can afford, from their earnings in the summer, to keep themselves until the visitors return. I won't say that they all enjoy an opulent standard of living, this must be far from the case, and no doubt many of them would take up temporary winter employment on the island if they could. But most of them are forced to vegetate, and to an outsider the relaxed tempo of life is noticeable almost as soon as he sets foot on the island. There are few anxious looks, but much kindness and courtesy. People move, cars drive more slowly. There is time for gossip and good cheer. There is freedom from the rat-race that prevails over the water.

There is no doubt, either, that a positive sense of freedom arises from the fact of living on an island. Not only are the people free of the harassing, cog-like existence on the mainland, but they have a strong sense of belonging to a community which is small enough for them to make a personal contribution. Many of them know every lane and village in the island and in their mind's eye they carry around with them a picture of their home: the rough diamond, the turbot, the bird with outstretched wings. This is very satisfying and as well as a strong feeling of security it confers on the inhabitants a sense of identity which "overners", as they call them, people from over the water, do not possess.

If the island scenery were flat and uninteresting it might feel like a prison from which people would be glad to escape. But there is so much variety—a view, so to speak, to suit every mood—that I cannot imagine anyone ever leaving the island because he wanted to look at something different. This variety certainly enhances the atmosphere of freedom, coupled with the shape of the island with its sixty miles of coast and the panoramic views from so many vantage points that an aerial map of the entire surface could almost be plotted without once leaving the ground. The long coast means, of course, that the sea is within smell and practically within sight wherever you are and in a place like this it is continually at the back of your mind, forming a sort of under-surface to your thoughts. In the village street of Freshwater, for instance, which is now the biggest shopping centre outside the towns, I am saved from the aggravation which rows of shops tend to arouse in me by the thought of the nearby sea pounding in Freshwater Bay or spreading like glass across the Solent. Magnificent seascapes are within reach wherever you go and, owing to the diamond shape of the island, as the sun gets lower different effects of light and shadow are visible on each of the four coasts.

As for the towns and villages, the countryside and the coast, there is a great deal to explore and the atmosphere by the sea and inland changes so quickly, ranging from innocent domesticity to the most forlorn desolation, that quick trips by motor-car are really no good at all. Every few miles you will miss something unless you get out and

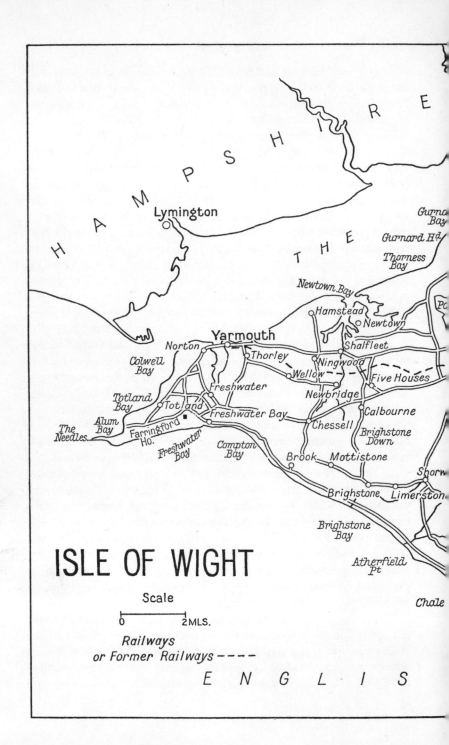

ISLE OF WIGHT

Scale

0   2 MLS.

Railways
or Former Railways - - - -

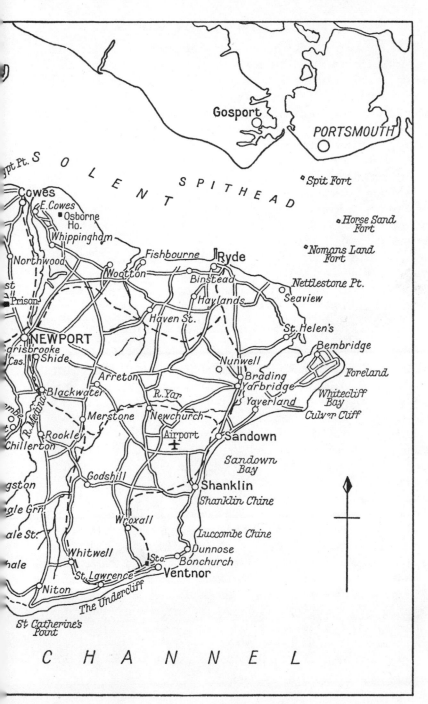

Gosport

PORTSMOUTH

ᵖt Pt. S O L E N T

S P I T H E A D

Spit Fort

Cowes
E. Cowes
Osborne
Ho.
Whippingham

Horse Sand
Fort

Nomans Land
Fort

Northwood

Fishbourne

Ryde

Binstead

Nettlestone Pt.

Wootton

Seaview

st

Prison

Haylands

Haven St.

St. Helen's

NEWPORT

Bembridge

arisbrooke
Cas.
Shide

Nunwell

Foreland

Arreton

R. Yar

Brading
Yarbridge

Blackwater

Yaverland

Whitecliff
Bay

mb

R. Medina

Merstone

Newchurch

Culver Cliff

Rookley

Airport

Sandown

Chillerton

gston

Sandown
Bay

gle Grn

Godshill

Shanklin

ale St.

Shanklin Chine

Wroxall

Luccombe Chine

hale

Whitwell

Sta.

Dunnose
Bonchurch

St. Lawrence

Ventnor

Niton

The Undercliff

St Catherine's
Point

C H A N N E L

B

walk, and practically no walk in any direction is disappointing.

One of the charms of the island is its lack of uniformity and a pleasant way to describe the scenery would be to choose some high spot here and there and describe the view from the top. But for readers who have never been to the island this would be confusing and it is better perhaps if we embark at Lymington and do the round trip— Lymington rather than Portsmouth or Southampton because the approach to Yarmouth plunges you at once in the authentic island atmosphere. As the ferryboat pounds slowly past the mudflats beside the twisting Lymington river the Solent opens up and there is a fine view to westward of the Needles just emerging beyond Heatherwood Point with Tennyson Down, like a stranded whale, in the background. Yarmouth lies ahead to the right of low, wooded hills: a compact little town clustering with sharp-gabled roofs round the tall church tower, with the yacht haven to the west, bright with activity and colour in the summer-time, battened down in winter, an arching bridge over the broad estuary of the western Yar, not many trees, rather flat countryside backed by grassy hills and a great sense of space.

Having landed, you cross the bridge—formerly a toll had to be paid here: 6d. each, proclaimed a notice, for a "car, hearse, litter, omnibus, stage coach" and, charming touch, "other like vehicles"—and you are now in West Wight, itself almost an island, cut off from the rest by the broad, sluggish waters of the Yar which rises close to the shore at Freshwater Bay. Inland, this little peninsula is mildly undulating and not very remarkable. But the coastal scenery is varied and some of it magnificent. It gets steadily more imposing as you drop down from the north-east towards the Needles: first, the wooded slopes west of Yarmouth (where, one November morning, Charles I spent a chilly hour waiting for a boat to take him as a prisoner to Hurst Castle), then the broad smooth sands of Colwell, a summer playground, then Totland, cosy, but wilder and flanked by a steepish headland. Last, on this coast, comes Alum Bay, an amphitheatre of towering rock, in all seasons rather forbidding, backed by the sheer coloured cliffs and shut in to the west by a vertical wall of chalk, 300 feet high, which ends in the massive blocks, or sea-stacks, of the Needles. In each of these bays, covering a distance of under four miles, the atmosphere is different, so different that when I was a child the Totland-addicts and the Colwell-addicts hardly ever mingled.

On the south side of the peninsula, facing the Channel, again there is a complete change. The north was slightly hermetic. Here everything is on a grand scale, open and free, splendid unspoilt scenery for miles and miles: the great bulk of Tennyson Down, green-capped chalk dropping sheer to the sea, topped sometimes with mist, where gulls wheel like animated snowflakes, the bright, tight semicircle of Freshwater Bay, then the Back of the Wight as the islanders call it where, a few miles further on, the chalk suddenly stops and a double band of low brown cliffs and paler sand sweeps away to the south-east with barely a single building visible and the only sounds, the cries of birds and the steady chant or roar of the sea. All this is utterly unspoilt. The beaches are open with not a man-made structure and behind the cliffs slope fields with sparse, wind-tilted trees towards wooded hills inland. From several points in this part of the Wight there are panoramic views. From Tennyson Down, the whole of the western island, the Solent and the opposite coast are visible. Inland and three miles further east, you can take a charming walk through pine woods from Brook Hill House and reaching the Long Stone view a further wide section of the Wight planted between the two waters.

Further still, towards the southernmost point of the island at St. Catherine's, the coast becomes more broken and forbidding and the black concave bowl of Blackgang Chine with its trickling stream looms above the sea. But the "awful and gloomy scene", as old writers described it, can only be viewed as a whole from the sea or the shore, and the shore is practically inaccessible now owing to landslides. Instead, a tourist attraction has been devised on the cliff-top: rock gardens with gnomes fiddling and playing cards round toadstools, a maze, model villages, distorting mirrors, the skeleton of a whale and a path which leads you half-way down the chine and then stops. But from here the gloom and horror is amply confirmed. Between Chale and Blackgang towering black cliffs have slipped bodily down and lie, forlorn as a slag-heap, by the deserted shore. From a distance there seems to be no vegetation and no life. Everything here is precarious, about to fall or already fallen, and the observation platform in the chine gardens shows a ruinous scene.

The landslip of 1928 blocks progress along the road past Blackgang, and instead you turn back to the route over St. Catherine's Down, through Niton and into a tunnel of green flanked by gnarled trees swamped with ivy and waterfalls burbling down rocks. This is the famous Undercliff, the terrace, a quarter of a mile wide, which slipped in bygone ages from the cliff behind and sprawls to the water's edge like a melting chocolate ice topped with angelica. Behind, but screened from the road, rear the chalk downs that are massed in this corner of the island.

Here the coastline eastwards to Ventnor is very picturesque with low, turfed cliffs, bluffs and daggers of rock where a path meanders as far as the town. Ventnor clinging on three levels to the hillside below towering St. Boniface Down is aggressively Victorian and some of the buildings are hideous. But summer with its trees and subtropical flowers breaks up the severity, the crowds on the short sandy beach add colour and movement and Ventnor, like a painted old lady, breaks into a seductive smile.

Beyond Ventnor there is more wild scenery compressed in a narrow crumpled strip below the downs, at Bonchurch every hollow, almost, sheltering a neat Victorian villa with sloping lawn. Then Dunnose, a blunt headland, rears darkly and behind it the main road to Sandown and Shanklin flows down in elegant curves through a wide and smoothly shaped valley, very like the approach to Eastbourne from Beachy Head, until the majestic curve of Sandown Bay, flanked at the far end by the white Culver Cliff, opens to the view. To stress that these two major holiday resorts are twins the island Tourist Board publishes identical brochures for both. But there is a difference, all the same. Along the sea-front, Sandown parades large hotels and boarding-houses backed by the red brick of the sloping town, while in Shanklin a single line of gabled houses tapers off to the west below a red sandy cliff which leads to the famous chine. These two places flowing into one another hold the sunshine record for the whole of the British Isles, and their position at the centre of this glorious bay with its long lines of curling rollers makes them a paradise for holiday-makers.

At Culver Cliff, which is the end of the central chalk ridge running right across the island from Tennyson Down, you reach a main vantage point from which to survey the scenery in this eastern extremity of the island. Below you lies Bembridge on the wooded peninsula of the Foreland which looks green from 300 feet up but on the ground is in fact fairly heavily developed, and immediately at your feet the sea foams in a crescent on the ledges at Whitecliff Bay, a small, sharply curving, unfrequented spot with broad sands and a sprinkling of dilapidated wooden sheds. To the north like an iridescent appendix gleams Brading harbour, so called because in olden time the sea extended over the valley of the eastern Yar and right up to Brading village which now lies a couple of miles inland. If you go down into the harbour the first thing that is likely to meet your eyes is a flurry of sand from the dunes, and in the off-season, when the only sign of nautical activity is the picturesque black-and-white timbered yacht club and row-boats stacked in the sun-lounge of the Royal Spithead Hotel, you will find it a forlorn little place, not improved by a row of antique railway carriages which serve as beach huts on the opposite shore at St. Helens, or by St. Helens itself which straggles austerely down a hillside above grassy dunes and common land. From the same Culver, however, you can look inland right across to Ryde on the north, Dunnose on the south, and westwards as far as Arreton and Newport, and a very pleasant, open, verdant scene it is.

From that height few buildings can be seen between Ryde and St. Helens, but on the ground, moving northwards from Brading harbour, you come shortly to Seaview. In summer the place expands considerably with boats and babies and the tourist literature speaks of a "strong continental atmosphere" in a town "vibrant with matters nautical". In the off-season Seaview dreams away the time, slightly sloping to the sea, heavily built up with smart-looking houses after the First World War, densely packed by the shore with picturesque stone and white-painted buildings and flat sands, half a mile wide when the tide goes out, curving northwards round Puckpool Point.

Seaview is much loved by certain families that go there year after year. Ryde, on the other hand, inspires more respect than affection. Seen from Brading Down, a highpoint on the central ridge about four miles inland, it appears as a mass of red rubble below the Solent which spreads in a narrow, pale blue band across the picture. The worst that can be said about Ryde is that it is not typical of the island, but a place where you can feel sunk and lost in those urban surroundings so familiar on the mainland; the best, that it is clean, friendly and spacious. The approaches are a shock, though. Modern council houses and bungalows litter the high ground behind the town, while lower down Victorianism comes into its own with massive, sash-windowed, yellow brick monstrosities and small-scale pseudo-Osbornes with towers from which nothing can be seen but roofs and chimneys. Down they lurch, those memorials to delusions of grandeur, to the splendiferous shopping street and then to the front with the long pier that acts as a sluice-gate to the island, the boating lake, the bandstand, public gardens and a broad esplanade. Along the front all is elegance and if Ryde were planted in Sandown Bay I would like it well enough. But to me its position opposite the clutter of Portsmouth harbour, facing north and wide stretches of sodden sand does not compensate for the tourist-industry atmosphere.

Westwards along the coast, though, which is somewhat inaccessible here, there is a long stretch of low wooded hills and fairly unspoilt countryside. There is not much character to this area. It is just ground with things planted on it and one of the things is modern Quarr Abbey, built in the Byzantine style of pale pink Belgian brick with much ingenious decoration and a bulbous tower. Architectural connoisseurs nod qualified approval, but exactly why is not clear to me: the abbey looks as though it made marshmallows, not monks. Close to Quarr is Fishbourne, a smiling little creek where the car ferry lands, and further on, its big brother Wootton. Old-time writers spilt a lot of ink on Wootton and its bridge, mill and mill-pond. But these felicities are now largely obscured by the hideous red brick village which confronts you beyond the bridge. Sweep this away, then go further down the creek and you will be happy enough in summer, basking on the roof of your house-boat with red sails drifting by.

The next area of the Wight, just east of the Medina river, contains East Cowes, Osborne House and Whippingham church with farms and a lot of tangled copses. East Cowes, a dismal place but the main manufacturing centre, concentrated after the war on making ships and aircraft, but in the late fifties these industries had to be largely abandoned and, after a serious five-year depression, are now replaced by marine and general engineering, hovercraft and smaller boat building. Nearby, just out of the town, is Osborne House, built to provide Queen Victoria with the seclusion which Windsor, Buckingham Palace and the Brighton Pavilion lacked. You should not be put off by the outward appearance of this Palladian mansion designed by the Prince Consort, but go inside. There you will find the Queen's private apartments furnished exactly as she left them, and I should not be surprised if one day the modern taste for clinical austerity in the home gave way to a passion for lush, crowded interiors such as you find here. Personally, I like walls sagging with pictures, pedestal vases and things under glass domes. They stimulate the imagination in a way that the lounge at London Airport never can. But even if you don't agree, the grounds at Osborne are really lovely, particularly the terrace gardens and the park sloping down to the sea.

Whippingham church, also designed by Prince Albert, is the third point of interest in this otherwise unexciting corner of the Wight. It has been much maligned, and a building which includes Norman and Gothic arches, a German lantern tower and rose windows copied from Notre Dame is easy to condemn. With all this in mind, coupled with the derogatory remarks of previous writers, I went to Whippingham, prepared for a shock. But inside I found the church attractive, at least as far as the nave and chancel are concerned, where the altar is backed by a lovely marble reredos of the Last Supper, given by Edward VII in memory of his mother. You are shown here the chair used by the Queen when she worshipped in this church (screened by a curtain from the congregation) and the broad pew occupied by her son. Many of the fittings were donated by the Queen, and the richness of the interior compared with other island churches underlines the royal patronage.

You can hop over to West Cowes on the ferry across the Medina, otherwise you have to go all the way into Newport down the east bank and up again on the west. This route is not very rewarding. The road runs broad and straight over flattish and somewhat congested countryside, past Parkhurst, which is not too savage-looking for a prison, past the radar factory, past brand-new bungalows, through steep, amorphous Upper Cowes and down more steeply still to the short esplanade. Can this really be the world-famous yachting centre? When the yachts are not there Cowes looks (but of course it isn't) a poverty-stricken town. The Royal Yacht Squadron's converted castle by the shore is drab and unpretentious. Drab, too, are the small hotels, the two-storey shacks and the massive concrete block of flats along the front. But in March, Cowes is just emerging from sleep. The paint-pots have only just come out, brushes heavily charged with blue and white. Down the winding main street—very narrow, very curious— old salts lope in dirty jerseys, the gleam still slumbering in their eye. But soon the flags will be out, the place will be poshed up, nautical folk will be swarming ashore from their board-and-lodging boats to the small butcher's (by royal appointment to George V), to the chemist and photographer (by triple royal appointment) where the *Britannia's* medicine chest is kept in the back shop, to a clothier's advertised as "yachting craftswoman" and to the grocer with his sign: "Coffee roasted daily, direct delivery to yachts." Ship's smiths, ship's outfitters, ship's chandlers, a carport below modern flats with the meaningful sign "Admiral's Wharf" and public lavatories shaped like the stern of a ship insist that in season this is the yachtsman's Mecca. But surely, you may say, such trivial signs are not needed to remind one of the fact? Isn't there a permanent glitter about Cowes after all the money that has been spent there? No, indeed there is not. In 1808 someone wrote that the lower parts of the town were narrow, irregular and crowded—they still are, and if the local grocer has built a marble palace it must be in Fiji, it is certainly not here.

Westwards again past Gurnard Bay, which has a short, sandy beach, lots of wooden huts and a grass headland convenient for caravans, you come to five miles of low-lying coast which is inaccessible except on foot, where there are no seaside resorts, no villages and hardly a single house. Newtown, lying half a mile inland in the centre of this area with its lagoon and creeks running in all directions, was once an important place visited by ships of 500 tons burthen, and in the town hall (still standing amid green fields) the burgesses elected two members to Parliament. But long ago Newtown harbour silted up and today 100 acres of marsh and woodland have been made into a Nature Reserve where, following a trail mapped, marked on the ground and documented in an attractive leaflet by the County Council, visitors, shedding the twentieth century as they go, can observe a profusion of wild life and plants; oyster catchers, for instance, curlews, terns, green and great spotted woodpeckers, yellow hammers, turtle doves, the flowering sea lavender and thrift, wild roses, the painted lady and holly blue butterflies.

As for the interior of the island, it is not too much to say that it forms an artistic whole. I mean that, almost wherever you go, you are satisfied with what you see. There is good proportion, great variety and completeness. You don't want to shift hills, or valleys or woods to make a more pleasing picture—they are in the right place already. This applies particularly to the southern half and the north-eastern section bounded by the Medina on the west and the line Newport–Culver Cliff on the south, in other words to the whole island except the top left quarter. The countryside there is on the whole too flat to provide anything but small-scale pictures: the broad, reedy western Yar, a village street or a delightful park with an old stone manor house sited in a sheltered spot. But elsewhere in the island it is the downs which determine the whole character of the

scenery: the main chalk ridge, seldom falling below a hundred feet
and in places much higher, which runs across the island and the
separate conglomeration of chalk in the south-east which provides the
highest point in the island at St. Boniface (785 feet), and a series of
deep bays and scarps on the inland side of the downs. From the lower
slopes of the main ridge between Freshwater and Newport, where
there is a very pleasant drive with the contours of the hills perpetually
changing, you look down on the northern plain and the Solent beyond.
East of Newport, Arreton and Brading downs provide further
panoramas: the south downs in the distance, the sea gleaming in a
narrow strip ahead with Shanklin church spire outlined against it, a
lush valley below with the eastern Yar winding through it, patch-
work fields, the village of Newchurch nestling on a little tree-topped
mound and, further west, Merstone stringing out beside a country
road.

But I should not like anyone to think that to view the Isle of Wight
all you need do is climb the central ridge and keep travelling along
it. There are the bays and bastions of the south downs and, bursting
out southwards from the main ridge, are innumerable crests, spurs
and sudden precipitous humps. Through the gaps between these
features and sometimes over them wind narrow country roads, some
with a tendency to peter out in a farmyard. Tarred surface? Well,
the map says so, but that is not quite true. Red dust is an essential
accompaniment to exploration. It is exceedingly worthwhile, though.
There are some ugly villages, and their names sound ugly—Rookley
for one, Chale for another—but many of them are pretty places in
memorable positions, Brading, for instance, reputed to be the oldest
village in the island, whose charming street with old cream, whitewashed and brick houses spreads like an Alice-band across a low brow
at the foot of Brading Down. At the top of the street is the beautiful
church and beside it the comical town hall, a diminutive building ᴜn
stilts, with one room above and the stocks and a sort of shed marked
"town jail" below. Most of the old villages are built entirely of stone,
though, obtained from the quarries at Binstead which supplied material
for Winchester Cathedral and some of the cottages consist of a mixture
of stone and chalk slabs which weather to an attractive green, brown
and grey. Most of them are thatched and they straggle or cluster, often
centred on a church, beside the island roads, looking extremely demure
and peaceful. Some of the villages are show-places; Brighstone in

open, undulating country, brilliant with flower gardens; Godshill with half-timbered cottages huddled on a steep mound beside a large church with a fine perpendicular tower and more cottages at the foot of the hill. Calbourne, with ancient church and vicarage and a mere handful of cottages nestles in a wooded cleft off the Freshwater–Newport road. Mottistone displays a fine L-shaped manor house close to the village green. All these and many more of the island villages have obviously changed little through the centuries, and the County Council guards them jealously from reckless development. Advertisement hoardings are also carefully controlled. A petrol pump, if that, is all you will see in the way of modernity. Some of the villages have no shops at all, others only one. In this whole area of the Rural District, which comprises half the island, there are 23,000 people and about 50,000 acres. Can you wonder that there is peace and charm in the interior of this island?

The charm, though, I regret to say, stops short of Newport, the capital, which lies in the centre of the island on the Medina river with its quays, cranes and busy traffic. Newport does not dream with thatch and red-capped gnomes and here the rural idyll is shattered. It is a dusty, rather shabby business town with no pretensions to the picturesque and when there I can never forget the factories, the breweries and the rows of yellow-brick terrace houses. Where, one wonders, have most of the ancient buildings vanished to? Because the town is very old and eighteenth-century prints show an intriguing maze of leaning gables and curious alleys. I suppose they were swept away in Victorian times and the town then emerged in this new guise, which is neither ancient nor modern, but a haphazard mixture of both.

Since the town was never much more to me than a back-drop for subjective experiences, it is these which hover in my mind now, as memories going far back into childhood. There was a small shop in the High Street where, on holiday, we bought freshly cooked crabs and having never seen one before and thinking it horrible I asked plaintively: "Which bit is it we have to eat?" There was a time when we went to see the film of Noel Coward's "Cavalcade", that moving record of a middle-class family from the Boer War into the 1930s where there was a toast at the end with glasses raised to England and peace. This puzzled me as I thought we already had peace. "Why did they drink to peace?" I asked my father as we came out. "Because", he said—and what a surprise to see that cheerful man suddenly so solemn—"because enduring peace is something there's never yet been in this world". As we drove back past moon-lit fields and sleeping villages to Totland I remember well that a nameless apprehension crept into me, the first crack in my vision of a paradise on earth, time-less, romantic, alas unreal, a vision that was to be finally shattered by a hoarse-voiced ex-corporal already in power in Germany. This is my most powerful memory of Newport.

Above Newport, however, looms Carisbrooke Castle, its high curtain wall rearing above the chalk hill on which it so comfortably sits. This is one of the most impressive clusters of Norman and medieval buildings in England, well cared for today after sorry neglect in past centuries, and the hub of island life for long ages when independent or semi-independent Lords and Captains lived here and the massive walls provided the only shelter in the whole island from marauding enemies. At Carisbrooke, where the Norman conquerors threw up their first stockade, where Isabella de Fortibus, the Lady of the Wight, held semi-regal state, where French cut-throats roamed the walls seek-ing in vain for entry and Charles I endured imprisonment, this brief survey of the island ends and history begins.

II

EARLY HISTORY

OVER August Bank Holiday no less than five thousand people a day visit Alum Bay to view the famous and unique coloured sands. Some of them may wonder how they arose. They may even ask themselves other questions. When, for instance, did the Wight become an island? Why the curiously truncated rivers, and why the rapid succession of cliffs which are so different in texture?

To all this geology supplies answers, and I will reproduce them because the island is well known as a geologists' paradise and here coherent history can really begin not with people but with rocks. Geological evidence is so accessible that along the southern coast you may dislodge something with your stick that throws a clearer light on ages long before the advent of man than any amount of research in island records can give you on, say, the life of the people in the fifteenth century. It is an odd fact. Is it peculiar, I wonder, to the Isle of Wight?

Millions of years ago, when water covered most of southern England, the island was part of the mainland. All its rocks are sedimentary, that is, they were deposited in layers in remote ages when the island was either the bed of a huge river or covered by shallow lagoons—more likely lagoons, because the oldest stratum called the Wealden, which consists of dull blue or blackish clays and is visible along the shore from Compton to Brighstone Bay, contains the bones of reptiles and the remains of timber and plants.

After the Wealden series was deposited it is thought that the level of the area sank and the erosion of nearby land surfaces built up further layers of great thickness on top of the Wealden. These new beds are called the Lower Greensand, the Gault and the Upper Greensand, and just to make matters more confusing, the green in the lower stratum is noticeable only on fresh exposure to the air, but then turns brown, white, yellow or grey. Only one bit has stayed green, the ferruginous sands which account for the dark colour of Blackgang Chine. Elsewhere along the southern coast where the Lower Greensand is visible, for instance at Atherfield, it is a dirty mottled colour. The Upper Greensand, consisting of light greenish to blue-grey sandstones, is seen along the Undercliff and forms the forbidding mass of rock which overhangs the road.

The Greensands would no doubt have stayed happily in place if it had not been for the Gault, the villain of the piece, which lies at varying depths over the whole area of the island. The Gault is impervious clay and in the south as well as the north it has become slippery (hence the local name "blue slipper") from the water which drains here towards the sea, so that wherever the strata above it have shown an appreciable tilt they have gone slithering downwards. The terrace of the Undercliff must have been formed in this way long before recorded history, but landslides still recur, the last major one being in 1928 near St. Catherine's Point when the old road between Blackgang and the Undercliff was cut. The Gault plays havoc with the north coast as we have seen, and inland, too, you come across a ploughed field sometimes with an unploughed hump across it where the soil has slipped and formed a fold.

So much for the earliest beds deposited aeons ago. But then the area sank yet further beneath the sea out of reach of erosive deposits and another process began. It is hard to realize that chalk is an organic product and harder still when you gaze at the sheer mass of Tennyson Down. But these trillions of tons derived from minute bodies produced by planktonic algae far below the surface of the sea. In this way the chalk ridge running across the island and originally stretching westwards to the cliffs of Studland was formed. In it flint was embedded, formed by the deposition of silica dissolved in sea-water around sponges which then grew profusely on the sea floor. At Scratchell's Bay just east of the Needles, which can only be seen from the sea, a 200-foot concave arch of chalk is beautifully striped with this flint in broad parallel bands.

After the deposition of the chalk, geologists deduce a kind of jack-in-the-box effect. The area rose, then sank again, and further masses of sand and clay were deposited—the Eocene rocks. Then the area rose once more. On top of great thicknesses of sand and coloured clays (red, purple, dark blue, brown and yellow) thrown down in the Eocene period, more clays, sands, marls and limestones were deposited in the following Oligocene age, and these particular beds are found nowhere else in England. Both the coloured clays and the later strata are all represented at Alum Bay, and when you look at those rainbowed cliffs—from a boat, a quarter of a mile offshore at sunset is best—you can picture their deposition in an age when the climate of the island was tropical and crocodiles and tortoises waddled amid waving palms.

As you face Alum Bay and its coloured sands rising above the shore you are confronting no less than six geological strata: the Osborne beds on your left at Headon Hill, all in a horizontal position and belonging to the Oligocene period, then the vertical Eocene strata which supply the colour, thrown up in some great convulsion long ago, the Barton Clay, the Bracklesham Beds, the Lower Bagshot Sands, the London Clay, the Reading Beds, and finally, a seventh stratum curving away towards the Needles, the massive chalk.

It was in those remote ages, long before man appeared, that the island, though still part of the mainland, assumed something of its present shape. As the land rose and the coast of Britain came into being, the Isle of Wight is thought to have been about five miles at its nearest point from the shore, embedded in an oblong stretch of land that now lies beneath the sea. To the north, roughly where the present Solent runs, was a great river, the Ancient River Solent, which rose in about the middle of Somerset with tributaries coming from Devon and Gloucestershire. This river flowed south-east through Poole Harbour, a mile or two south of Bournemouth where it was joined by the Lower Avon, and then along the bed of the present Solent till it turned south-east again past the "island" and joined the sea some seven miles south of where Brighton now stands. At that time, the island rivers—the West Yar, the Medina and the East Yar—did not rise within the modern perimeter, but several miles to the south of it, and northwards they all flowed into the great River Solent. That helps to explain the phenomenon of the West Yar which we see today: a broad shallow stream which at one time must obviously have carried a much greater volume of water than it now does.

In Palaeolithic times, therefore, about two hundred and fifty thousand years ago, there was no Isle of Wight. The same Early Stone Age men roamed here as in the rest of the country, over land probably 600 feet higher than it is today, a sparse population which in the island has left no fossilized bones, but only implements in the shape of rough flints called hand-axes. Much later, the Ice Age descended when extreme cold alternated at long intervals with a milder climate and a diorama in Carisbrooke Museum depicts a shaggy mammoth, whose fossil remains have been found in the island, standing in forlorn majesty amidst a meagre vegetation of coarse grass and stunted birch trees.

But then, about twenty thousand years ago, after long aeons of time, the ice began to retreat northwards and the Isle of Wight became covered with thick forest. River settlements were developed and then, as the level of the sea rose, abandoned for higher sites. Fishing became possible and some sustenance could be got from wild fruits. Then, possibly about seven thousand years ago, the great chalk ridge, which at that time extended in a continuous belt from Freshwater to Studland in Dorset forming a narrow barrier between the Solent River and the sea, was breached and the modern island came into being. This is not thought to have been a sudden event, but a slow process brought about by the sinking of the river bed and the steady scouring of the tide.

Man, in his new-found island, would now be gazing over a surface not so very different from what it is today, except that the downs would be a little higher, the valleys not so deep and the coastline would still extend further south. One can imagine him somewhat indifferent to his gradual separation from the mainland. Wild life on the island was plentiful—horses, oxen, deer and wild boars—and pre-historic refuse heaps revealed by landslides near Bonchurch show that in the Neolithic period, or Later Stone Age, this varied diet was supplemented with winkles and limpets. Axe-heads and pottery discovered in the island show, too, that its inhabitants, who could still walk over dryshod to the mainland at low tide, were not bypassed by the so-called Neolithic revolution which by successive invasions brought the technique of farming from the Middle East, the use of pottery and greatly improved implements.

So in the island for about a thousand years we can picture an almost stagnant life, with settlements near the coasts because of the fishing or on the southern downs which were easier to clear of vegetation. In due course, bronze, that other invention from the Middle East, also arrived.

Then, around 1900 B.C., as in other parts of England, the Beaker people—so called from their distinctive pottery—arrived and mated their no less distinctive round skulls with the indigenous long-headed variety. The Beaker folk, also known as the Alpine Race, do not seem

31

to have settled permanently in the Isle of Wight, but they stayed long enough to mislay some of their pots and use others to bury alongside their dead. One of these was found at Nunwell near Brading, beside it a round-headed skull with teeth ground flat by a gritty diet. This gentleman, or lady, ranks as the oldest islander of whom anything remains.

With infinite slowness from about 500 B.C. waves of immigrants from Europe, including the Belgae from northern France, brought the Iron Age culture to England and with it a slightly different way of life. All the features of this age which archaeologists have noted in England also apply to the island: hill-top forts (there is one at Chillerton Down south-west of Newport), an increased consumption of domestic animals, the cremation of the dead and the use of a single heavy stone to crush grain. These were variants, but hardly advances in culture. When the Belgae arrived, though, somewhere around 100 B.C., this virile and intelligent race brought some new ideas with them— chariots and coinage—and no doubt they quickly established their authority in the island. But they were not to enjoy it for long.

The Belgae themselves, by their flourishing trade with the Roman Empire, soon attracted predatory eyes to Britain, and when conquering Gaul Julius Caesar had received reports of England's climate and resources. It is unlikely though, that his first inconclusive raid on Kent in 55 B.C. or his second in the following year aroused more than a ripple of curiosity, if that, in the Isle of Wight, and nearly a hundred years were to pass before the Roman Eagle was planted at Carisbrooke and the inhabitants were gazing wide-eyed at the skirted warriors who told them that their island was henceforth to be called Vectis.

Then, in A.D. 43, the long and bloody tale of the Roman conquest began: the stubborn resistance of Caractacus, the endless raids and clashes from the Wash to the Severn, the rebellion of Boadicea followed by fire and merciless slaughter. All this, with its romance and its savagery, was spared to the Isle of Wight. Resistance there would have been useless and the island fell like a ripe plum to Vespasian as he was advancing westwards within a few months of the first landing.

For nearly four hundred years, the island, like the rest of Britain, supported a veneer of Roman civilization above the original, primitive economy. If people on the mainland came to accept the occupation

32

and ultimately to feel pride in their citizenship of a world-wide empire, this must have been doubly so in diminutive Vectis. Here there were no tribal wars or forays from across the border to disturb the calm. Apart from a Roman fort at Carisbrooke built probably as a centre of resistance to Saxon raids in a later century, there are no traces of early military camps or roads. Vectis may have been used as a place of retirement for wealthy officials or deserving generals. Of the five hundred or so Roman villas unearthed in southern England, six are in the island, the finest of them, discovered in the nineteenth century on Brading Down, consisting of twelve rooms forming three sides of a courtyard, with a bath block, central heating system, a 50-foot hall with tessellated pavement and frescoes depicting mythical scenes. Here and on the nearby Undercliff where hoards of coins and other remains have been found the Romans could enjoy vistas and a climate reminiscent of their home, and the islanders living in their primitive huts would look up to them as law-givers and protectors, well content with the long years of peace on the rim of the Roman world.

But under the pressure of Central Asian hordes pressing upon their homeland the Saxons were already invading Britain before the Romans left, and by the middle of the fifth century A.D., when the legionaries had gone, the country was falling into their power. Succeeding years told a horrid tale of treachery and slaughter, abetted by the Picts and Scots. Marauders in the first place, the Saxons went home to tell of rich booty beyond the seas and soon they were returning in swarms to conquer and settle. They fought the Britons, they fought amongst themselves and eventually from a chaotic scene there crystallized a number of kingdoms, each under its warrior chieftain. Around the year 500 a number of blood-soaked barbarians hoisted themselves into the seats of power, in Wessex (a broad strip along the south coast), and in Sussex, Kent, Essex and Mercia, comprising the Midlands.

These rulers had to consolidate their power before turning their eyes elsewhere and for some years the Isle of Wight was unmolested. Then, about A.D. 530, the West Saxons Cerdric and Cynric invaded, killing many men at Carisbrooke, and united the island to Wessex. As it added no strength to the kingdom their object was probably booty and a desire, prevalent among Saxon chieftains, to confer land on their faithful warriors. Four years later, after Cedric's death, the same idea occurred to his nephews Stuf and Wihtgar; it is from the

C

Newtown Bay

latter that the name Wight is derived and also Carisbrooke, then called Wiht-gara-burh, where Wihtgar lies buried.

For the next hundred years, while on the mainland Saxon fought Briton with unabated fury, history is silent about the Wight. Then in 661 we hear that the King of Mercia's son Wulphere devastated the island and no doubt for political reasons ceded it to Aldewach, King of Sussex. Twenty-five years later, Aldewach was killed in battle by Caedwalla of Wessex who promptly reincorporated the island in his own kingdom. But this was not the end of the matter. As long ago as Roman times Christianity had been brought to Britain, a British and a Saxon Church had developed, but in the days of St. Augustine Ethelbert of Kent had been the only Christian ruler. Now the new creed was spreading rapidly and many a king and kinglet was pondering conversion, not solely for spiritual reasons. Among them was Caedwalla. Wessex, he had already decided, should be a Christian land capable of alliance with Christian partners and the scenes of idolatry which he saw in the island filled him, we are told, with wrath. He resolved that the pagans should be slaughtered to a man and the island replanted with Christians.

Fortunately for the inhabitants this was not carried out. Caedwalla gave three hundred families to Bishop Wilfrid of Selsey for treatment as he thought fit and merely slaughtered the rest. No doubt in his eyes the new faith demanded some victims. Thus Christianity came to the Wight in the guise of a new terror and the first natives were baptized at Brading where, it is believed, the first church was built.

For many centuries yet, however, the Gospel was at variance with events, though during the two hundred and fifty years of Viking raids and settlement in Britain the Isle of Wight seems to have fared better than the mainland. It had the distinction of the first recorded Danish attack, unsuccessful apparently, which occurred in A.D. 787. But for over a century thereafter the small island waited in suspense while its fate was decided on the mainland where the Danes ravaged northern England and, creeping further south, became locked in mortal combat with King Alfred of Wessex. There was one isolated raid on the island, lovingly recorded in the Anglo-Saxon Chronicle, perhaps because it was the only known occasion when Alfred's new long galleys played a part. In 896, three years before he died, six Danish ships put men ashore at Brading. A fierce fight ensued during which nine of Alfred's galleys appeared to cut off the retreat. The Danish survivors embarked, but harried by the English they ran aground on the mainland where they were captured and hanged at Winchester.

After the death of Alfred there was peace for many years under his son Edward whose effective sway covered all England south of the Humber, and though in the time of his descendants there was sporadic fighting on the mainland no Dane seems to have set foot on the island. But from 978 to 1016 ruled Ethelred the Unready and his folly is reflected in the annals. Ethelred tried to buy off the Danes. They took the money, and went on raiding. In 981, using the island as a base, they burnt Southampton, massacred most of the populace and carried off the remainder into slavery. The English fought a pitched battle with the Danes in Essex, were defeated, and the enemy raised his price. Again Ethelred paid, in ten years, the fabulous sum of £50,000, and for half that time the island suffered a veritable martyrdom from Danish raids and periodic occupation. Waltheam, probably the modern Werror on the west shore of the Medina estuary, was destroyed, and other villages—villages for the sole reason that there were no towns.

For the next eighty-five years, until the Norman Conquest, the islanders lived in misery, their home a defenceless prey to marauders. Sweyn, King of Denmark, descended. Danish pirates appeared again under Edward the Confessor, prior to ravaging Sandwich. Early in 1066, King Harold's half-brother Tostig, who had quarrelled bitterly with him and fled to the Norman court, appeared with a fleet off the coast, but was defeated before he could use the island as a base for invading England.

For the islanders, reduced by these long trials to the level of harried animals, the Norman Conquest, bringing firm rule and security at last, came none too soon. With England in his grasp, Duke William declared dividends to his friends and to William FitzOsbern, Grand Seneschal of Normandy, senior commander at Hastings, kinsman and boyhood friend, he gave the lordship of the Isle of Wight, in complete independence subject only to his suzerainty. FitzOsbern promptly dispossessed the Saxon landowners in favour of his own followers, the Fitz-Sturs, the Fitz-Azors and one Hugh de Oglandres whose descendants after nine hundred years still live in the island today. Then he bethought him of security—after all, the Danes were still active—roped off a 20-acre area at Carisbrooke, built the gigantic mound on which the Norman keep now stands and started constructing earthworks. Finally, there were deeds of piety to be performed. A priory was built at Carisbrooke and six island churches, with their tithes, were bestowed on the Abbey of Lyra which he had founded in Normandy. That done, the Lord departed to fight in Flanders and the islanders saw him no more.

FitzOsbern was killed in an overseas battle and was succeeded by his truculent son Roger. He found rebellion against the Conqueror more to his taste than cultivating the garden isle and for this he paid with life imprisonment and forfeiture of the lordship. William was once again sole master and to Carisbrooke he now came to teach a lesson to another potential rebel, his half-brother, Odo, Bishop of Bayeux and Earl of Kent, the same man who in years gone by had supervised the weaving of the Bayeux tapestry. From the Wight, we are told, Odo had organized an expedition to Rome where he hoped to be elected Pope. This William could not allow. Odo was intercepted in the Channel, brought back to Carisbrooke and there, in a kind of log cabin which was so far the only structure, confronted with his furious brother. As none of his henchmen dared lay hands on a Prince of the Church, William arrested·him in his capacity as the Earl of Kent, shipped him off to Rouen and left him in a dungeon until he, William, was on his death-bed.

The next appointment to the lordship of the island, made by Henry I soon after his succession, reflected Norman family quarrels. His title had been contested by his elder brother Duke Robert and the rivalry was not settled till he crossed the sea and defeated him in Normandy. One of his supporters in the fight had been Richard de Redvers, descended from an illegitimate son of the first Duke of Normandy, and to him was now granted the lordship. It·stayed in his family for nearly two hundred years.

Enjoying the same absolute powers as the first lord, the de Redvers and their successors the de Vernons have left scant record of their rule. The fact that Richard's son Baldwin gave a charter to Yarmouth, the first town in the island to receive one, shows that in the early Middle Ages the West Wight had greater commercial importance than the East—the opposite of the situation today. In the cultural sphere the balance was redressed by Baldwin's founding of the Abbey of Quarr, close to the coast about a quarter of a mile east of Wootton Creek. Here, in eighteen years, amid sheltering elms and surrounded on two sides by water, was built a stately edifice which for four hundred years until the dissolution of the monasteries was the chief civilizing influence in the island. It was peopled with Cistercian monks from the monastery of Savigny in Normandy and with ample grants from Baldwin and his son William became very prosperous, owning some of the..finest lands in the island. The Lord Abbot was a spiritual peer, sitting in the Upper House, and younger sons of the gentry competed for appointments as treasurer, steward, chief butler or rent-gatherer. In the fifteenth century the Abbot had his own ships for conveying wine which by royal permission he was allowed to import duty-free, and he was also allowed to fortify his northern shore-line against invaders. The sixteenth-century topographer Lambard wrote querulously that "the inhabitants of this island be wont to boast merrily that they neither had amongst them monks, lawyers, wolves nor foxes, yet I find them all save one in a monastery called Quarr", and the monks were certainly not averse to poaching on the neighbouring manor of Ashey. But it was a calamity for the island when in 1537 the Abbey was dissolved. Soon after, the buildings were bought from the Crown by impious overners who demolished them and sold the material locally. In the island today there may still be houses including stone from Quarr, but all that remains of the Abbey itself is a length of wall joined to one end of a barn, gleaming greyly not far from the modern pink-brick monastery.

By siding with the Empress Maud against King Stephen during the disputed succession after Henry I's death, Baldwin de Redvers all but sacrificed the lordship of the island. He was besieged by the King in Carisbrooke Castle (where he had built the Norman keep and curtain walls) and when the water supply ran out was forced to surrender. After a period of exile, however, he was allowed to return to the island and died, reinstated in the lordship, in 1153.

For another hundred and forty years the same family held sway, building priories, all of which were dissolved in the time of Henry V, and conferring much land and tithes on various abbeys in Normandy. French monks came over and established cells to supervise the cultivation of their lands and the transmission of revenues. Newtown, then known as Francheville, was given a charter and also Newport, then consisting of a recently founded settlement which no doubt owed its existence to the seat of government at nearby Carisbrooke.

Meanwhile the castle was growing beyond its original defensive purpose and by the end of the thirteenth century domestic buildings provided an opulent contrast with the primitive dwellings of the islanders: a hall, a great chamber and four other rooms, a great kitchen, a larder, bakehouse, brewhouse, granary, two chapels, a prison, stables, a barn for hay and forage and a gatehouse flanked by tall towers containing more rooms. Practically every trace of these buildings has now disappeared, but here, with ample cellars for her wine and a tank of live fish for her table, resided in great state Isabella de Fortibus, Countess of Albermarle, Lady of the Wight, the last direct descendant of Richard de Redvers and the last of the independent Norman rulers. Her reign was a fitting close to a period in island history which leaves no record of calamity or invasion. She set Newport on its feet by making the town a borough, granting commercial privileges and giving the freehold of much land to the burgesses. Unfortunately all her direct heirs died before her and on her death-bed she was persuaded to sell the island to Edward I for 6,000 marks, in modern money perhaps half a million pounds.

Since the thirteenth century, therefore, the Isle of Wight has been a possession of the Crown—so today there is no need to worry about passports, as some people still think they should! For another two hundred years almost the island was governed by wardens chosen locally or else by English Dukes and Earls possessing hereditary rights. Sometimes they could not even be bothered to view their domain, but ruled through stewards varying in zeal and honesty.

The change was not an improvement from the islanders' point of view. A year after their absorption into the realm of England, King Edward declared war on France and enemy raiders appeared in the Channel. There was an invasion scare and for the first time in living memory watch and ward had to be kept in the island. That was bad, but the King also demanded that seven of the island knights should fight for him in his war against Scotland, which had declared itself an ally of France. With memories of the peaceable Isabella the seven found this too much and, arguing that they were not bound to do the King service beyond the Solent, they simply refused to go.

There is no record of a punishment; perhaps there was none. At any rate, a few years later the islanders again showed their independent spirit when Edward II tried to foist his favourite, Piers Gaveston, on them as absolute lord. The local landowners would have none of him, and so the young Gascon was removed and given the governorship of Ireland instead.

There now began, under Edward III, the greatest calamities in island history since the Danish invasions.

III

FROM FORTRESS TO FAIRGROUND

FOR several reasons which, even at this distance of time look fairly respectable, Edward III decided on war with France. In 1340, passage over the Channel for his army was won at the sea battle of Sluys. But the French had also been planning the invasion of England. Baulked of the larger prize, they descended instead in that same year on the Isle of Wight, landing at St. Helens where a stiff fight ensued in which the leader of the home forces was killed at the head of his men.

This was a serious event. From now on, enemy raids might be expected at any time, at almost any point, and to meet them promptly before widespread damage was done was impossible in an under-populated area with no regular soldiers of its own. The people were also poor and could ill afford time off for martial exercises. Some years later, Froissart wrote: "The Isle of Wight has space enough for the residence of a great lord, but he must provide himself with all that he may want from the adjoining countries or he will be badly supplied with provisions and other things." Nevertheless, throughout the reign of Edward III, strenuous efforts were made to organize an effective defence. Lords of manors were called on to provide men-at-arms and bowmen and these were supplemented by a hundred fighting men from the City of London. No one was allowed to leave the island except on urgent business, and those that did, in anticipation of fur-ther raids, forfeited their property. In later years, a more rigorous system was imposed when the island was divided into districts called "centons", each commanded by a centoner, who was usually a leading landowner, with a lieutenant and a troop of a hundred or two hun-dred men. The watch and ward was tightened up, warning beacons installed, and to help spread the alarm when it was given "hobblers" were appointed, so called because they were mounted on small horses, or "hobbies".

Alas, none of these arrangements could prevent an enemy force from landing; the best they could do was to drive it out before the island was turned into a desert. In 1377, after the population had been further reduced by the Black Death, the French landed in force at Yarmouth, burned it and Newtown to the ground and then advanced inland to Newport. Goaded by the fear of being cut off from their ships, the invaders made a great slaughter and from the north coast terrified women and children are said to have sought refuge in the massive tower, thirty feet square, of Shalfleet church. Inland, the populace streamed to Carisbrooke. The French reduced Newport to ashes, all but the church, and then advanced on the castle. Here fortune favoured the defenders. An enemy body was ambushed and killed in a defile thereafter known as Deadman's Lane and from the walls of Carisbrooke one Peter de Heyno immortalized his name by shooting the leader of the French with a cross-bow as he was creeping up to reconnoitre. Under the Constable, Sir Hugh Tyrell, Carisbrooke withstood what was to prove the last serious siege in its history, but then stalemate ensued. The castle could not be captured; the French could not be driven from the island. Finally, they agreed to go after exacting a humiliating fine of a thousand marks.

Newtown never recovered from this devastating raid; two hundred years later, Yarmouth and Newport were still suffering from the effects. When a commission inquired in 1559 into the decay of the capital, the burgesses ascribed it to the burning by the French. These facts bring home to us the slenderness of island resources in bygone days, the precariousness of its economy and perhaps, too, the fatalistic mood of the inhabitants. From the mid-fourteenth century onwards they were never free for long from the fear of invasion. Why bother to rebuild what could again be so easily destroyed? The records show that their main concern was to protect what they still possessed and when the French returned in 1402 they gave a good account of themselves. The marauders landed 1,700 men, burnt two villages, but then, as we are informed by the parish registers of Northwood near Carisbrooke: "On hearing that the people of the island were assembled, they made haste to their ships and returned home."

Two years later, they were back again with a thousand men, but "the islanders coming upon them took away their booty and made many of them leave their own carcasses for a booty to the islanders. Yet the French would not leave it so, but a while later, as having got new spirits, they cast anchor before it and required the whole island to be delivered up." The last sentence seems to be a variant on a story that the French demanded a subsidy in the name of King Richard and Queen Isabella. This piece of high-flying impertinence fortunately found the islanders well prepared and resolute. King Richard, they pointed out, was dead. But if the French cared to land, they might do so unopposed, have six hours to refresh themselves and then accept open battle. This chivalrous offer the marauders declined. Once more, however, in 1417, they landed and boldly declared they would spend Christmas in the island. The inhabitants thought otherwise and drove them off with heavy loss before they could embark their booty.

This, until the time of Henry VIII, was the last of the French raids. But the people were by now in a miserable state and it was not helped by the absentee Lords who had wider ambitions than to govern the island realm. If we look at a chart of the Houses of York and Lancaster, soon to be involved in the Wars of the Roses, we see that many famous names on both sides possessed the lordship of the island: Edward Duke of York, who died smothered on the field of Agincourt, his widow Philippa, Duke Humphrey of Gloucester, Edmund Duke of Somerset and Lord Scales, brother of Elizabeth Wydville, Edward IV's Queen. I doubt whether the islanders ever saw these august personages, and certainly they never cast eyes on their "King" whom the feeble-minded Henry VI crowned with his own hands in 1444, during the era of the good Duke Humphrey. The lucky monarch was the royal favourite, Henry Beauchamp, son of Warwick the Kingmaker, and a later engraving shows him kneeling with his crown slightly askew, a wisp of hair escaping from it and an anxious look on his face. But he need not have worried. In the following summer the young man died at the age of twenty-two in Worcestershire, leaving only one trace of his kingship in the island, an inn-sign, common for many centuries thereafter, representing a bull derived from the supporters to his coat of arms.

The islanders, in any case, had graver matters than the royal puppet on their minds. Four years later, after the good Duke had come to a violent end and Richard Duke of York, father of Edward IV, had been given the lordship, they addressed lengthy petitions to King and Parliament. "Please it unto youre most excellent grace to be enfourmed how that your isle of Wighte stondeth in the grettyst juperdye and daunger of any parte of youre Realme of Inglond . . ." Through pestilence, war and unjust exactions many inhabitants had fled to the mainland. Too few were left to defend the island. Carisbrooke Castle was in a miserable state, "nother stuffed with men and harneys, nother with gonnes, gonnepowder, crosse bowes, longe bowes, arrowes, longe speres, axes and gleyves as such a place suld be in tyme of Werre . . ." Hence, with rumours that the French planned renewed descents, the inhabitants were discomfited and amazed, seeing the feebleness within themselves. And there was another grievance. John Newport, the Duke's steward who ruled in his name, had been dismissed from office, but refused to go. Instead, he was parading about, calling himself Newport the Gallant and Newport the Rich, stealing corn, pocketing the royal revenues and making piratical raids on peaceful Solent traffic. It was said that, having bled the island white, he was proposing to sell it as his personal possession. The islanders wished to be rid of John Newport. But whatever happened, they needed "gonnes" (a new thing in those days, much admired) and able-bodied men to defend the island when the French returned. All this prompted the royal response: *le Roi s'avisera*, and nothing, it seems, was done.

As it happened, the next calamity to befall the island did not come from a French landing, but from the reverse operation, an expedition to France. Edward IV's brother-in-law, Lord Scales, had been given the lordship in 1466, "in special tail, to his heirs male, the whole Island of Wight with the Castle of Carisbrooke and all other hereditaments, by fealty only for all services." It is said that he took much interest in the acquisition and his rule was probably benevolent. But in the Wars of the Roses, which did not touch the island, the temporary triumph of Richard III cost him his life and he was murdered at Pontefract Castle. The new king abolished the custom of conferring the lordship with hereditary and territorial rights and it was never revived. From now on, the island was administered by governors, and after Bosworth and the accession of Henry VII the honour was returned to the Wydville family in the person of Lord Scales's younger brother, Sir Edward Wydville. He promptly performed a ruinous deed. For decades the English grip on France had been weakening and in a quarrel between the Duke of Brittany and the French King he saw a chance of dealing a counter-blow. Henry VII, who visited the island about this time to inspect the defences, is thought to have given his approval, whereupon Sir Edward organized an expedition of forty island gentlemen and four hundred yeomen to fight for the Duke. In the summer of 1488 they set off in four ships from St. Helens gaily clad in white coats

43

with broad red crosses. To give the enemy the impression that the foreign allies were more numerous than they were, some of the Duke's men in Brittany adopted the same dress. This stratagem proved ineffective. The whole force was cut to pieces at the battle of St. Aubin and only one boy got back to the island to tell the tale. The loss of so many vigorous young men was a terrible blow and was little eased by statutes intended to attract immigrants to the island. It was described at this time as "desolate and not inhabited, but occupied by beasts and cattle".

For another hundred years, until the defeat of the Spanish Armada and the establishment of English naval supremacy gave security to the island, its whole life was inhibited by the fear of invasion. In those days, one successful attack in a lifetime was enough to keep the people demoralized, for they knew that the English navy was not strong enough to ward off a determined invader and in an unexpected onslaught soldiers sent from the mainland would arrive too late to be of use. Constant military training and the formation of an Isle of Wight militia merely underlined the feeling that they lived in a "frontier place", as they called it, where the fruits of many years' hard work might be destroyed in an hour.

So it was on a still poverty-stricken island that the French again descended in July 1545. This proved to be the last and largest invasion which the island has ever suffered. In the previous year, Henry VIII had declared war on France, crossed the Channel with an army and captured Boulogne. Now the French returned the courtesy, heading for Portsmouth with 220 ships and galleys carrying 6,000 troops. Their arrival was not unexpected. Henry himself was encamped on Southsea Common and ordered his fleet to engage the enemy. In the narrow waters of Spithead the French could not deploy their superior numbers and the battle was inconclusive. They then decided to lure the English ships into the open by ravaging the Isle of Wight. In all, about two thousand men were put ashore at Seaview, Bembridge, Shanklin and Bonchurch. But the islanders, reinforced by some thousands of men from Hampshire, were ready for them and all were repulsed in two days. At Bonchurch, where the French landed two parties, one to press forward along the Newport road and another to fill casks with fresh water, there was a hot skirmish with many slain on both sides. A French nobleman in full armour, at the head of men protecting the water party, was caught and battered to death by a boorish fellow who

44

ignored his appeals for ransom. A fat captain from Hampshire was overtaken on a hill and calling vainly "A hundred pounds for a horse!" vanished into enemy hands. On Bembridge Down good work was done with cavalry, barricades of farm carts and ambushes. From Seaview, after destroying a small fort, the French hastily re-embarked and from Sandown they were driven off to a man. In all, it was a famous success for the islanders, and it resulted, soon after, in the erection of solid forts at East and West Cowes, Yarmouth and Sandown. From now on, also, each parish was ordered to keep a gun, a "falconet of brass or iron", which in most cases was kept in the church or a shed built on to the tower. None of these pieces was ever fired in anger.

Though unsuccessful, the French attack did nothing to raise morale and until the latter part of the sixteenth century island conditions were bad. The Reformation had brought great demoralization in church affairs and in some parishes there was no resident minister whilst others were served by laymen. Carisbrooke had fallen into decay and the district of Castlehold, which was exempt from the jurisdiction of the borough, swarmed with vagabonds. Newport was in a parlous state, with filthy houses and unpaved streets. Before long, the plague would almost decimate the population and the road to the cemetery be blocked with carts carrying the dead. Nothing was manufactured in the island and exports of wool and corn were flagging. Nevertheless, in the early years of the Great Queen, a spirit of jollity amidst squalor spread amongst the people, helped by the appointment to the captaincy of a typical Elizabethan sea-dog, Sir Edward Horsey, who came, rubicund and genial, to his new post with a welcome reputation for dealing in drastic fashion with French Channel pirates. Disdaining the crumbling grandeur of Carisbrooke, he went to live at the rambling manor house of Haseley where one Mistress Dowsabell, comely widow of the infamous merchant who had demolished Quarr Abbey, kept house for him at the rate of a couple of bullocks and eight sheep weekly. She also consoled him for a wife absent in France.

Sir Edward was very popular. He helped to stock the island with hares, promising a lamb to all who brought in a live one, took care of the defences and patronized sports and celebrations: hawking, coursing, bull-baiting and time-honoured customs at Newport. Among these an old ledger book records a picturesque ceremony. In those days, the forest of Parkhurst stretched for five miles from the west bank of the Medina to Newtown creek and was so dense in places that squirrels could run the whole distance from bough to bough without touching the ground. Though the forest belonged nominally to the Captain of the island, the people had free right of pasture there, and on the Saturday after May Day the bailiffs of Newport appointed a crier to ride with a minstrel about the town, "a pretty company of youth following them", to summon every citizen, on pain of forfeiting a green goose and a gallon of wine, to attend next day before dawn at the forest to fetch home may. There the keepers offered the bailiffs small green boughs in token of the pastoral rights. Then the citizens cut down boughs and marched home with them, "the commoners before, the keepers following them; next, the minstrel and morris dancers; after, the sergeants with their maces; then the bailiffs, the guns and chambers going off after a triumphant manner until they come to the corn market, where they shew such pastime as they like to make." The boughs were used "to refresh the streets", being placed at the doors "to give a commodious and pleasant umbrage to the houses, and comfort to the people passing by". Meanwhile, the bailiffs prepared themselves with speed for morning prayer and afterwards went with their wives to dinner. At the end of the day, it was prescribed that the wives of leading officials should walk abroad, two by two, with the morris dancers and the minstrel playing before them— "and so return, in like manner, somewhat before evening prayer, passing the whole day in good company, mirth and honest pleasure."

The days of honest pleasure, when Mistress Dowsabell herself liked to dance through the fields after a drum and pipe ended abruptly when her protector died of the plague in 1582. His successor, Sir George Carey, great-nephew of Anne Boleyn and in high favour with the Queen, was a strait-laced martinet. Only the castle was good enough for him and only three ladies on the island were thought fit company for his wife. Young men were abjured to "utterly leave the play at bowls, quoits and other unthrifty games" and train themselves for defence. With the Spanish threat developing this was not unsound. But Sir George went too far. On reaching years of discretion, youths now had to take an oath of fealty to the sovereign in a new form, swearing to defend the island against the Queen's enemies, keep it "always true English", obey the Captain, obey the appointed centoner, denounce traitors (in other words Papists), and maintain their arms in good order. Instead of unthrifty games, competitions in the use of the pike and arquebus were organized. Four hundred pounds were raised from the island gentry for defence and workers conscripted to help repair Carisbrooke Castle. To stop food and people leaving the island a system of permits was introduced, which had to be paid for. Business suffered and the inhabitants saw no reason why their Captain should line his pocket with illegally exacted payments. Resentment simmered. No wonder, they grumbled, he was consuming wine at the castle at the rate of four hogsheads a week and always had a concert of "wind and still music" to accompany his meals. . . .

But then, in July 1588, the beacons flared along the southern coasts of England. The Spanish Armada of one hundred and thirty ships had been sighted off the Lizard. In the island, two thousand well-trained men, over a fifth of the population, stood to arms with muskets, bows, pikes and halberds. Every creek and inlet was guarded; every down had its watch and ward. The Spaniards, it was rumoured, meant to capture the island and use it as a base. For five days their massive ships ploughed their way up-Channel pursued by the English fleet that had put to sea from Plymouth Sound. Early on the morning of the 25th, after both fleets had been becalmed for a time near Portland Bill, they appeared off the south coast of the island. Then the wind suddenly dropped again and heavy firing broke out between the ships across less than 120 yards of water. The Spanish high turrets were badly battered and the ponderous ships tried to move closer together for protection. When the wind revived, both fleets moved slowly eastwards like stately clouds on the summer sea and vanished over the horizon—towards Calais where the Spaniards lost some of their finest ships, towards Gravelines where eight more were destroyed and then northwards, pursued and pursuers, on the nightmare voyage round the north of Scotland, where the English were forced to turn back for lack of food and the Armada sailed on through mountainous seas towards home. It was a great deliverance, greater for the Isle of Wight than for any other part of England, and on the night of the 25th, as it was getting dark, the Governor of Carisbrooke Castle wrote to London: "This morning began a great fight betwixt both fleets south of this island, which continued from five of the clock until ten, with so great expense of powder and bullet that during the said time the shot continued so thick together that it might rather have been judged a skirmish with small shot on land than a fight with great shot on sea." Not two of our men, he reported, had been hurt and both fleets had disappeared from view towards three in the afternoon.

Three months later, the island gentry, secure at last and eager for untrammelled enterprise, sent a massive petition to London, complaining of Sir George Carey and his absolute government in the island, "tending to the subversion of the law and to the taking away of the natural freedom of the inhabitants". But in fact this was the first time that they had enjoyed natural freedom for nearly three hundred years.

From now on, the island slowly emerged from its stagnant life as a "frontier place", and though for another century defence was taken seriously by authority, if not always by the islanders themselves, no serious threat of invasion came. A picture of the island under Elizabeth and in the early seventeenth century is given in a later chapter on Sir John Oglander. Manor houses sprang up. Humbler folk had their thatched, stone-built cottages with vegetable gardens. There were many small farms where wheat, barley, oats and peas were grown. Pigs fed on the acorns in Parkhurst forest. Large numbers of sheep roamed the downs. Wool, corn, butter, cheese (which the unappreciative called "Isle of Wight rock") and timber were increasingly exported. Cowes was growing as a victualling centre for the fleet, St. Helens as an anchorage. It was a time of steady progress under Captains who never seemed perfect to the islanders, but largely left them to manage their own affairs.

The Civil War enhanced, if anything, the prosperity. There was no fighting in the island and many people came over to escape the turmoil with the result that rents and profits soared. Almost from the start it was obvious that active partisanship was ruled out in the Wight. If the whole island had declared for the King it would have made no difference to the outcome and as it happened the islanders were divided. Most, but not all, of the gentry were royalists. When Portsmouth was besieged by the Roundheads they tried to run in supplies, but desisted upon threats. With the fall of Portsmouth and Southampton they could do nothing but pray for the King and live with great caution at home. For the people as a whole, from self-interest if not from inclination, were for the Parliament. In 1642, the royalist Captain, the Earl of Portland, had been removed from office and in an attempt to arrest his wife the mayor of Newport had laid siege to Carisbrooke Castle, aided by the crews of parliamentary ships. But the Countess had acted like a Roman matron, threatened to fire the first gun herself and had finally been given safe-conduct to the mainland. Under a new Captain, a Committee of Safety composed of tradesmen then

48

Shalfleet
(overleaf) *Yarmouth*

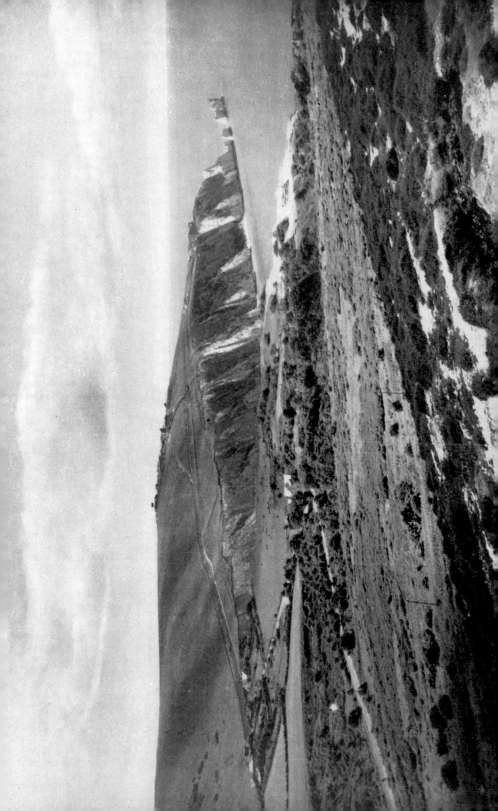

ruled the island. An atmosphere of mingled puritanism and suspicion descended in which parents were fined for allowing their children to play on Sundays and harassing restrictions on trade and free movement were imposed. The gentry eyed their new rulers with fury, but remained outwardly calm.

To this island, simmering with faction but increasingly prosperous, came Charles I on 14th November, 1647. The Civil War was over, but no settlement was possible between a Parliament insisting on constitutional government and a King convinced he was born with a divine right to rule as an autocrat. It was his duty, he believed, to maintain his prerogative despite defeat in war, despite the fact that for five months he had been the prisoner of an army which had refused to disband and was itself at loggerheads with Parliament. Charles had no intention at this time of fleeing overseas to save his skin. With each week the potential martyr in him was becoming stronger. But if he was to save his cherished principles of kingship he would have to regain independence. This he did not possess in the hands of the army. There were rumours, indeed, of a plot to murder him. So on the night of 11th November he escaped with three companions from Hampton Court where he was held prisoner and rode through torrential rain to Tichfield House by Southampton Water.

From there he sent two friends to Carisbrooke Castle to sound Governor Hammond's sympathies. He had reason to hope that this man would protect him. Though Hammond had fought for Parliament he had become critical of Cromwell and had been glad, a few months before, to retire to the Isle of Wight. Moreover he was a nephew of the King's chaplain at Hampton Court. But Hammond—who can blame him?—was non-committal and on being conducted back to Charles at Tichfield he only promised that he would do what he could for him. This was not enough, but Charles had never intended that Hammond should be brought to Tichfield, his whereabouts were now known and it was impossible to make other plans. So the King crossed to Cowes and from there was taken at once to Carisbrooke where comfortable rooms were put at his disposal and for some weeks he was free, attended by members of his own household, to go where he liked in the island and see whom he pleased.

Now, if ever, was the time to escape abroad. But this was not the King's purpose, and news probably reached him of growing discontent in the army which showed that in England all was still in a state of

D   49

flux and flight would be premature. In any case, when Parliament heard where he was, Hammond was instructed to confine him to the Castle, restrict access and have his bedroom door guarded at night. The King now saw that he had exchanged one prison for another.

The life was not exactly harsh. Charles was treated with all respect. By day he could walk within the perimeter of the walls and later a bowling green and summer-house were provided for him in the east barbican. He could write and read to his heart's content, and found intellectual exercise in religious discussion. Above all, he could still hope that from the turmoil over the water would emerge a clear opportunity for him to resume power with his principles vindicated. So the royal prisoner was calm, even cheerful, invariably courteous to his captors, like a man enduring a brief sentence before freedom returns.

It is hard to say when the realities of the situation first dawned and his attitude changed. By the end of 1647 he had reached deadlock in negotiations with Parliament. The growing power of the New Model Army under Cromwell, its rejection of all compromise, all forces in the country that favoured even a modified return to the old régime may also have told him that history was entering new paths where there would be no enclave for a throne, no place for himself. The contrast, too, between his own inactivity and the surging tide of events in England must have been painful in the extreme. Within a few months he was ready to attempt escape.

A game of cat-and-mouse was already going on between his friends who received letters from him in cipher and parliamentary agents who intercepted and decoded them before passing them on. In January 1648, Hammond was warned from London that there were plots to "convey away the King". Two more warnings were sent to him in the following months. But when Charles made his first attempt on the night of 20th March Hammond still knew neither date nor details, and instead of a royal martyr there might have been an exile in France —but for one fateful error of judgement. At this time, Charles was lodged on the first floor of the building, now in ruins, facing the entrance to the castle. The plan, prepared by Firebrace, his faithful groom of the bedchamber, was for him to file through a window bar and escape to the curtain wall where a rope was ready to lower him and friends were waiting with horses at the foot of the wall to take him to a boat on the south coast. The King said a file was unnecessary; he knew he could get his head through the bars and, being a very small man and slim, he presumed also the rest of his body.

On the night of the 20th all was ready: the helpers, the rope, the horses, boots and pistols for the King, the boat. Charles began to squeeze his way out. Firebrace was waiting below. He saw the head emerge, but then, to his horror, all movement ceased. The shoulders were stuck. "I heard him groan," wrote Firebrace later, "but could not come to help him, which was no small affliction to me." Charles, indeed, only just managed to pull himself back into the room. Then he put a lighted candle in the window to warn his friends that he had failed.

The party dispersed unseen, but later, from captured correspondence, Hammond learnt details of the attempt. Firebrace was dismissed with others of the royal attendants, security was tightened up and the King moved to another room against the north curtain wall overlooking the main castle bank where, on a specially built platform, three sentries were posted night and day.

The rigours of confinement became more intense. His hair and beard were already turning grey and he now began to neglect his appearance. The previous £10 a day allotted for his maintenance seems to have been reduced. There was a lack of clean linen and even wine; he took to drinking two parts of water to one of sack. The solitude deepened. Later, when negotiating with the Parliamentary Commissioners in Newport, he pointed out to a friend "a little old crumpling man" in the street, "the best companion", said Charles, "I had for three months together in Carisbrooke Castle, where he made my fires". But he did not despair. On the fly-leaf of many books which he had with him at this time he wrote: *Dum spiro spero*—while I breathe I hope.

Other plans for escape were considered. One, which entailed exchanging clothes with a coal porter, was abandoned, but on 28th May a second attempt was made on the same lines as the first, this time with nitric acid, obtained by astonishingly devious means from London, to eat through the window bars. The acid did its work, the King was ready to climb out when a scuffle started on the bank below him. The rescue party was engaged with Hammond's men and it transpired that one of the bribed sentries had changed his mind at the last moment and warned the Governor. The King's friends only just managed to get away.

But now, after a mutiny in the army claiming "England's Freedom! Soldiers' Rights!" had with difficulty been quelled, parliamentary leaders were coming to see Cromwell and his Ironsides as a threat to all they had fought for. An accommodation with the King was favoured and, with the second civil war in full swing, Commissioners were sent to Newport to parley with Charles. For the last time a semblance of royal pageantry surrounded him: courtiers, a state coach, footmen in new suits with broad plate-silver lace, selected chaplains of his own (a great relief after the Puritan hot-gospellers who had plagued his life in Carisbrooke), a presence chamber in the grammar school where he lodged and a platform with canopy of state in the town hall where he met the Commissioners. All this was bought in exchange for his parole not to leave the island.

So to Newport, in late September—a town of many streets, noted a new arrival, but the buildings none of the best—came Lords and soberly attired Members of Parliament followed by a great influx of flamboyant Royalists. Their headquarters were the "George", a modest inn; the equally modest "Bugle" absorbed the Commissioners. To hold the protagonists apart some companies of foot had been provided, but proved unnecessary as the mood on all sides was hopeful. Never, before or since, has the island capital achieved such historic importance. To the opening session at the town hall Charles travelled the short distance from the grammar school in his coach of state. While the Ironsides in fury and in rags were sweeping all before them on the mainland, here, before the goggling islanders, the last tributes were being paid to the still unbroken tradition of monarchy. For six weeks at the town hall negotiations were spun out over a religious and political settlement. Tempers· were kept; a heavy sense of responsibility weighed on all. Finally, Charles agreed to a treaty which left him his crown but little else, and with the army triumphant over the water it was a dead letter as soon as signed. To the Commissioners he made a farewell speech: "My Lords, you are come to take your leave of me, and I believe we shall scarcely ever see one another again. But God's will shall be done. I thank God I have made my peace with Him, and shall not fear whatsoever He shall be pleased to suffer men to do unto me. . . ."

Two days later, the foreboding underlying these words was fulfilled. On 29th November, a wet and blustery day, rumours reached Charles at the grammar school that bodies of troops were being landed in the island. By evening the numbers had risen to two thousand. Some were reinforcing the guards in Newport, while others were at Carisbrooke where their grim-faced officers threatened the Governor of the Castle with immediate death if he did not preserve discretion. A royalist officer bringing these ominous tidings to the King found that conditions at the grammar school had changed drastically within a few hours. There were now guards outside the building, guards at the windows inside and more guards at the King's door itself. As they were half suffocating him with their burning torches the guards on the door were persuaded to move further off. An anxious discussion ensued between Charles and his three remaining attendants. They were convinced that the army had arrived to seize his person. What else were these troops waiting for in the pouring rain, in the peaceable Isle of Wight? Charles did not doubt it. But what could he do? To prove that escape was still possible, one of his friends, the Duke of Richmond, now disguised himself in a voluminous cloak and with the royalist officer who knew the password succeeded in passing the guards at the door. They must have been very stupid, for they even let the two men return. So there *was* a way of escape; it was worth trying. But this was the last chance.

The King did not take it. His words, recorded on the following day by the officer, Captain Cooke, showed resignation rationalized into a belief that he must do nothing to imperil his treaty with Parliament. He would not budge. Cooke asked a hypothetical question. If a boat were waiting at Cowes, and horses, and escape proved easy, as he himself had shown it could be—what would His Majesty do then? "They have promised me," said Charles, "and I have promised them. I will not break first." Did this refer to the parole he had given the Parliamentary Commissioners? The army, protested Richmond, not Parliament, was now in control. At any moment it might inflict on him a speedy and absolute imprisonment.

Then Charles spoke his last word. Did he realize that it was irrevocable? Did he know that this was the parting of the ways, and that he was choosing the short road to martyrdom? Probably not. More likely he was aware only of nervous exhaustion, the pouring rain, Newport stuffed with troops, dangers on every hand. He could not face them. "As it pleases God," he said—and announced his intention of retiring for the night.

At dawn he was arrested by army officers who hustled him into a coach and conveyed him, with only a few personal servants, to a point west of Yarmouth. From there a boat took him to Hurst Castle which juts out into the Solent from the mainland. The final scene in Whitehall lay exactly two months ahead.

The execution of the King had a pathetic sequel. In 1650, his two younger children, Elizabeth aged 15 and Henry aged 10, were brought to Carisbrooke so that, in the official language, "they might not be objects of respect to draw the eyes and application of people towards them". They were well treated and "Master Harry", as he was called, was released after two years and allowed by Cromwell to go to his mother in Paris. But within a month of her imprisonment the Princess Elizabeth was dead as the result of a chill caught when playing bowls with her brother. She was buried in a coffin with a plate marked simply "E.S." in a vault under the old church at Newport, and its whereabouts remained unknown until 1793 when it was discovered during repairs. It was only in the 1850s, however, when a new church was being built under the patronage of the Prince Consort, that Queen Victoria commissioned a marble monument and a stained glass window as a tribute of respect and in memory of her sufferings.

From the time of the Restoration recorded history dwindles off into the names of successive Governors, aristocrats who had little to do with the island, but were pleased enough to draw a salary of £1,000 a year which was not abolished until 1789, when the Governorship became purely honorary and the island was administered by local nominees. A hundred years later, when County Councils were first established, it was administered for a short time from Winchester, then acquired its own County Council. Meanwhile, the first years after the Restoration were oppressive. The Great Plague came to Newport in 1665 and after raging for a while stopped short of a house by the church, still called for that reason God's Providence House. There was a cantankerous Governor, Lord Culpeper, who threw innocent citizens into a wearisome dungeon at Carisbrooke and, until prodded into activity, neglected the defences. These, during Charles II's wars with Holland and France, were important. But though the Dutch fleet was twice sighted and the islanders mustered in full panoply of war they were not called into action, and after the defeat of the French at the Battle of the Hogue in 1692 invasion fears vanished from the island for a hundred years and the militia was virtually disbanded.

If you visit Yarmouth church you will see in a side chapel a life-sized marble statue representing a somewhat saturnine figure in full armour. This is Sir Robert Holmes, Irish soldier of fortune, Culpeper's successor, known to contemporaries as "the cursed beginner of the two Dutch wars" because, without a declaration of hostilities, he ravaged Dutch settlements off West Africa in 1664, crossed the Atlantic and seized New Amsterdam (which he rechristened New York) and, two years later, raided the Dutch coast, destroying ships and villages. Charles II was delighted, but to placate the Dutch first imprisoned him in the Tower before giving him the governorship of the Isle of Wight. The islanders liked him very much.

But Holmes was no proper symbol for them. For the next sixty years or so warlike pursuits receded and the islanders smuggled, fished and tilled the soil in peaceful isolation. Cowes was still growing as a naval victualling centre and ship-building was just beginning. But Brading, with its harbour and quays, was still an important place. Then visitors began to discover the island's beauties, the more robust explorers at first, followed by artistic folk, "bloods" and "macaronis".

Only one more trial lay ahead, the Napoleonic Wars, when invasion fears revived, defences were reorganized and—to the corruption of simple rustic manners, we are told—four thousand five hundred troops were brought over from the mainland. With three thousand inhabitants also under arms, this provided a density of one soldier to every three civilians. The island was one huge garrison. Enemy marauders intercepted vessels off the coasts and the Southampton–Cowes packet was captured entire. But there was no invasion and after the end of hostilities the island oyster began to open up. The founding of the Royal Yacht Squadron, a steamship service with the mainland, railways from London to the south coast, the building of Osborne and the arrival of Queen Victoria—all this increasingly turned the island into the playground which it has remained ever since. A spate of building development started. Ventnor was the first big holiday resort and its story is told in another chapter. Ryde, Sandown and Shanklin followed. Slowly the isolation of the little communities was broken down, though for some time yet the way of life remained more primitive than on the mainland. In the 1880s a dictionary of the Isle of Wight dialect was published, and though it seems doubtful whether there ever was a dialect peculiar to the island, many stories told in illustration of the words suggest a rural population of almost Arcadian ignorance and simplicity.

But population was climbing steadily, between 1860 and 1870 at the rate of a thousand a year, and by the early 1900s it had multiplied four times in the previous century. This, together with the annual flood of visitors, administrative uniformity and better communications tended to destroy local traditions, smooth out peculiarities and clothe the once individualistic islanders in the garb of typical English citizens. But they were not always so, and in the rest of this book some light will be shed on the island as it used to be, with its sparse and sprawling population, suspicious of strangers, warring sometimes amongst themselves, very busy about their arduous and by no means legal pursuits, so different in their way of life from the modern Vectensians that no part of the British Isles, one might say, has undergone a greater change in the last hundred years.

IV

WEST WIGHT AND THE BARD OF FARRINGFORD

FROM the network of streets that wind and twist over the western peninsula, the rows of red brick houses, the trail of aspidistra that fuses Freshwater, Totland and Colwell into one, Yarmouth stands charmingly aloof, with a distinctive atmosphere, clean, breezy, highly nautical, sedately old-world. Formerly the town was bounded on three sides by water, on the south by an arm of the sea as well as on the north by the Solent and on the west by the river estuary. Consequently it could only spread to the east and this it did very slowly so that today there are around four hundred houses compared with fifty-nine in 1766. The town is very compact and as you approach it over the bridge from Totland you feel you could almost balance it in the palm of your hand.

But this little place now devoted to pleasure and the yachting season has had a long and eventful history. It is mentioned in Domesday Book as Eremud which, in its more usual spelling Eremue, was a name interchangeable with Yarmouth for several hundred years. No doubt because of its strategic importance it was granted a charter in 1135 by Baldwin de Redvers, Lord of the island under Henry I, and this charter was confirmed by succeeding monarchs.

Perhaps the royal recognition was partly intended to boost the morale of the inhabitants, for they sorely needed it. The town was destroyed by the French in 1377 and again sacked in 1524 when the bells of the badly damaged church were carried off to France where it is said that they can be seen today in the church of St. Peter and St. Paul at Boulogne with the name Eremue still legible on the metal. After this second raid the present castle was built by Henry VIII to protect the town and the entrance to the river. Meanwhile, struggling to raise their houses from the ashes the inhabitants lacked spiritual comfort. In 1559 the town was too poor to support a priest, and even a hundred years later, though the church was adequate for the congregation, there was still no minister, but only a reader, a feeble old man who for the last seven years had been too weak in body and mind to perform his duties. "We want a Godlie preaching minister," declared the inhabitants in a petition, but in the same breath admitted that this phenomenon was a rarity and rarer still the money to support him. As a result, a minister was obtained, but his stipend had to be found outside the town.

From James I Yarmouth received a more comprehensive charter which made the town a borough and conferred a mayor and corporation, and a borough it remained until abolished under the Municipal Corporation Act of 1883. Fifty years earlier it had lost the privilege of sending two members to Parliament.

From these details we can see that as the main port of the island Yarmouth had greater significance than the mere number of inhabitants would seem to warrant, though judging from the records they were a sturdy breed, sailors and longshoremen with their own peculiar code of honour. From an interesting book by a local author, Mr. A. G. Cole, we glimpse the forebears of the Yarmouth men who today make boats, rigging or sails and help to man the lifeboat. In the last century many of them were smugglers, a hazardous trade which they pursued more from a thirst for adventure than in the hope of high profits which, at any rate in this part of the island, were not very large. The smugglers, we are surprised to hear, were a splendid type of men, self-respecting, patriotic, clean in their speech and neat in their dress. Not for one moment did they consider their trade disreputable. It seems to have been more like a game of catch-as-catch-can in which they and their opponents the coastguards tacitly observed certain rules. It was played mostly in winter. when the long nights and rougher seas were an advantage to the "free-traders". All went well so long as the coastguards stuck to their part of the bargain, which was to accept bribes with a good grace, patrol certain areas without excessive zeal, and on rough nights when, like as not, there would be much activity on the shore, keep firmly in their shelters. Maybe I exaggerate the tameness expected of the coastguards, but being billeted locally they could hardly sustain a war to the knife with the smugglers. At any rate, the fate of one man who offended against the code is on record. He was captured on a dark night, lashed up in a sail with one or two holes to breathe through, rowed out to a

French lugger and despatched to the Continent where he was unceremoniously dumped on a deserted beach. His family was informed by the kind-hearted smugglers that he had gone on holiday, but would be back in due course. . . .

The local worthies were at all times alert to protect their rights as they saw them and chief of these seems to have been the right to preserve the town just as it was, without alteration or improvement. They objected to the building of the breakwater which now forms the seaward side of the yacht haven because it prevented unrestricted access to the river estuary, and this was very important to the smugglers. For this project not a penny was forthcoming from local purses and the promoters had at last to appeal to the island public who, they declared, were their last resource and only hope.

For similar reasons there was fierce opposition to another much needed improvement, the construction of the Yar bridge in 1863. At that time, passengers from Yarmouth to the opposite side of the river at Norton, the only direct route to the West Wight, were transferred by ferry and so keen were the local smugglers to keep this part of the river open that no one professed to find a change desirable, despite the ferryman's peculiar rates: one penny for a working man and sixpence for gentlemen, the latter defined as persons wearing white collars. Probably few people in Yarmouth wore them anyway. But the bridge was built and later a long wooden pier was constructed for the use of steamers. To the Yarmouth sailors this was the last straw. It doomed their trade rowing passengers ashore, and the Corporation had the impertinence to build gates so that the pier could be closed after working time. But these gates blocked the sailors' access to the beach—or so they maintained. They warned the Corporation not to erect them. The Corporation went ahead. So the sailors took action. They "sold" their boats to friends and relatives so as to get rid of their seizable assets, and then smashed the gates to smithereens. The Corporation sued, obtained an injunction restraining further violence but could recover no legal costs. Then it put up another set of gates, slanted so as to provide free access to the shore. Everyone was satisfied and the event went down as a triumph for the people of Yarmouth who, being almost literally one large family with only one member on the Corporation, had in any case always looked on it with suspicion.

Yarmouth is a charming place now, but it must have been even

59

more intriguing a century ago with these robust individualists, its thatched cottages, the town wells where people drew water with a bucket and chain, the bakehouse where families sent their bread and Sunday dinners to be cooked, and a variety of customs, all of which have now disappeared. Most of them were not peculiar to Yarmouth. The Christmas mummers, acting their traditional play with the Bellman, the Valiant Knight and the Turkish Knight, performed all over the island. May Day was a universal occasion celebrated with country dances and a procession of small girls carrying garlands of wild flowers. Oak Apple Day, when boys wore sprigs of oak in their caps, was also kept throughout the Wight. But peculiar to the town was the annual fair held on 25th July, St. James's Day, St. James being the patron saint of the church. Devoted to the calling of the sea and much cast on their own resources, the people in normal times were well behaved and sober. Only on the fair days were the rules relaxed to allow a spot of rowdyism and tippling on the cheap beer then plentifully available, and, to show that the law turned a blind eye, a pole was hung out from the ancient town hall in the square with a stuffed glove on the end representing an open hand. This custom died out in the 1870s.

But Yarmouth has no need of these quaint occasions to underline its individuality. I have seldom met a town more cheerfully and purposefully different. To the east along the waterfront retired admirals pace invisible quarterdecks, and one large house named the Towers has a stone wall facing the sea with black squares imitating gun-ports still painted on it, originally to scare away the French. Close to the castle there is a pleasant inn named the George, once occupied by Sir Robert Holmes, Governor of the island and called Yarmouth's hero for his buccaneering exploits. There he entertained Charles II and there in 1799 George Morland, the artist, was arrested as a French spy by the over-zealous Isle of Wight Fencibles and frog-marched to Newport with a highly incriminating document: an unfinished sketch of a spaniel which they had found on him and took to be a map of the island. In the churchyard sleep many forebears of the present inhabitants, for Yarmouth families cling tenaciously to the town and look back with pride on the feats of seamanship and life-saving performed by their ancestors. Some of these are almost legendary now, the story, for instance, of a Yarmouth pilot who on Christmas Day long ago rescued a dismasted West Indiaman in foul weather off the Needles, but they help to maintain the seafaring tradition now centred on the lifeboat, which serves the whole of the West Wight and since 1924 has saved hundreds of lives.

For me many memories are bound up with Yarmouth: being towed over with a car in a barge behind a paddle-steamer before the war, gliding in summer towards the slipway past red sails slanting before the breeze, creeping in on a winter's evening with the mainland invisible astern and ahead the dully glowing windows of houses and the tall church tower looming in the semi-darkness. At all times I am glad to come back to the friendly little town, and this applies to the whole of the West Wight where I spent many holidays in childhood and have often revisited since.

This western peninsula presents itself in a variety of pictures. First, there is the West Wight of long ago, a wild place approachable on land only by rough tracks at Freshwater Gate. From time immemorial the people had lived practically cut off from the rest of the island, fishing, tending their flocks on the downs, occasionally as they ploughed disturbing an ancient burial-ground, when they would gaze in surprise at earth-encrusted ornaments, little knowing that they themselves were descended from the Jutish invaders who had once worn them. They had to be self-supporting and it was a hard life, but with the sea beating on three sides of their home never a monotonous one, and in their thatched cottages by the twelfth-century church at Freshwater, the only village in the whole area, they felt reasonably secure. At the fate of Yarmouth beyond the river, twice razed to the ground by the French, they could nod their heads and say: "That can't happen to us." On the east, the marshes of the Yar were better than any man-made barricade. Cliffs guarded them on the north and south. Only at certain points, Totland, Colwell and Freshwater Bay, could an enemy set foot and find room to deploy. These points were guarded and in addition, as part of the island defence, a watch was kept on the down overlooking the Needles.

Personal memories supply another picture. When I first saw the West Wight as a child, the watch and ward had vanished (though to be revived during the Second World War), the dense woods that once stretched from Freshwater to Totland had also gone and the old village was lost in a sprawl of Victorian development. The people no longer lowered themselves perilously to collect samphire and gulls' eggs from the cliffs, and alum was no longer dug at Alum Bay. I had been told about wrecks, but to my great disappointment they never seemed to occur. Almost the whole of the interior was one vast dormitory and shopping centre for the families that crowded to the beaches by day. The West Wight had become a playground.

But none of this mattered and still does not matter, because the coastal scenery is so splendid. Daily in bright sun—the sun always seemed to be shining—we trudged to the shore from the little apartment house that lay a mile inland and was always wrapped in mystic gloom. The contrast between its hermetic interior, cluttered with Victorian furniture, and the sense of freedom by the sea was extraordinary. Dusty plants in pots, heavy curtains, plush-covered chairs laced with cooking smells and the reek of linoleum fought and lost their battle with the ozone. Over this spotless dungeon presided an old lady (I thought of her as old) who had never been to the mainland and hardly ever, it seemed, left the house. In level tones, with extreme dignity, clasping her hands beneath an ample bosom, she told us overners of the sights which those seeking pleasure—suspect word!—might view on the island: the Needles lighthouse, the yachts at Cowes, Carisbrooke Castle. It was said, though it was many years since she had been there—not since she was a child, in fact—that the beaches on the south coast were nice for a picnic. So we piled into an antique taxi, a pre-1914 Delaunay-Belleville driven by a moustachioed cock-sparrow of a man, surged perilously round the traffic-infested roads and usually, on the driver's advice, landed up somewhere quite different.

But the sea coast was the mainstay of the holiday. We put up bell-tents on the blue slipper at Totland, bathed, sucked ices and made brushwood fires to boil kettles for tea. The coarse grass was full of spiders, the blue clay stuck to our feet, the shore was rocky, the water always seemed cold. But this was childhood, and consequently our love went out as far as our eyes could see: to the lighthouse at Hurst Castle with the brown curve of the mainland shore glimmering in the heat, to the Shingles Bank in mid-Solent flecked with wicked tongues of spume, to the great blue sea where paddle-steamers sidled over from Bournemouth to disgorge red-nosed trippers on the pier and liners glided past with gleaming white upperworks to send little wavelets plashing on the shore when they had gone. The feel of salt water and sand, of the sunlight, of hard-boiled eggs when they were peeled, of little breezes that sprang up and caressed the body, all this, day after day in a familiar scene that slowly seemed to become one's personal possession, conjured an enchantment that lay sparkling in the air and still tingled in the nerves at night.

Into glass tubes we scraped the coloured sands at Alum Bay (now provided in trays at the cliff-top for so much a dig), and saw a monument to Guglielmo Marconi where from a little shed he made wireless contact with boats in the bay and in 1897 established the first permanent wireless station in the world. We strode along Tennyson Down, westward to see a magnificent view of the Dorset coast, eastward to overlook low brown cliffs curving away in a mysterious haze towards St. Catherine's Point. We took a motor-boat from Totland and, fishing for mackerel, ploughed through the swirling eddies by the Needles lighthouse and gazed with awe at the huge concave arch of chalk with diagonal bands of flint at Scratchell's Bay, where razor-bills and guillemots wheel and puffins sit in solemn rows on ledges like white-bloused old ladies with black chokers. Further on, someone pointed to caves at the foot of the towering cliffs and said they were known as Lord Holmes's parlour and kitchen because he had once entertained his guests in one and cooled his wines in the other.

Any trips that took us close to the sea delighted me; excursions inland I considered a waste of time. In the gloom-filled island churches I set up my camera for time-exposures, but no music played, and outside in the sunlight gulls glided with their mournful cry, the foaming breakers crashed, at sunset a trail of fire like a blood-stained sword shot out from the Purbeck hills. Here was a loftier church, a ceremonial yet more sublime.

Today these coastal scenes still fascinate me, and the roads of Freshwater and Totland, though uninspiring, are friendly because they lead towards them. In thirty years there has been a good deal of building at Freshwater, but not much that is visible at Totland and the bay itself is resolutely the same, except that the bathing huts look smarter and the concrete esplanade has been extended and repaired. There never was, and I hope never will be, anything slick about this sea-front. Almost the only touch of modernity, the only change I can detect in all those years is a smart modern pilot-boat tied up at the pier. Three times a day, on average, after receiving a radio signal from a ship, one of the young Master Pilots comes down from the smart new house built for them on the cliff and the boat surges off with him to the rendezvous two miles outside the Needles. The pilot climbs on board the liner or tanker, a tricky operation in bad weather, goes to the bridge and there navigates the ship through the Solent and up Southampton Water—or, strictly speaking, advises the captain how to navigate, because the captain remains responsible.

The final picture which rises in the mind about this corner of the island is of Tennyson, the greatest man who ever made his home here and fittingly commemorated by the granite cross that stands to-day on the highest point of the down renamed after him. Judging only by his poetry, some readers may be in doubt about his stature. The high moral tone, the sentimental stories which many of his poems tell, their studied pictorial effects, the clanking symbolism, the legendary atmosphere—all this is somewhat out of tune with the present age and I must admit that, with exceptions, my own enthusiasm is more for Tennyson the man than the poet. A lot has been written about him, a great deal has been recorded by his contemporaries, and from it all a clear impression emerges of a very lovable, childlike and, despite his quirks, almost saintly character, comforter and oracle combined who, almost from the moment that he and his wife came to live at Farringford, turned this snug, tree-girt, sea-swept corner of the island into a place of pilgrimage where humble folk thronged to catch a glimpse of him and leading Victorians in all walks of life—politicians, artists, scientists, educationalists and churchmen—came as to a shrine for spiritual refreshment and intellectual debate. Tennyson held them all, by the force of an extraordinarily frank yet gentle personality, by his earnestness, his wisdom and his humour.

His *In Memoriam*, with its agonized reflections on the death of his friend Arthur Hallam, had struck deep echoes throughout Victorian society, and in 1850 Tennyson had been appointed Poet Laureate with the admiring approval of the Prince Consort. He had been in two minds whether to accept the honour, but, as he said, after drinking a good deal of old port at dinner had finally been nerved to say yes. In that same year, at the age of forty-one, he married Emily Sellwood, four years younger than himself and with her intelligence, firm belief in his mission as a poet, capacity for self-sacrifice and goodness of heart, the ideal partner. Whereas before his marriage he had complained of growing old and feeling miserable and anxious, he now told an admirer of his sense of a divine mission entrusted to him by God. He felt that his gift of poetry was an awful responsibility and that he was accountable for every word he wrote. Here was born that

Freshwater Church
(overleaf) Freshwater Bay and Tennyson Down

high sense of moral purpose, absolutely divorced from priggishness, be it said, which was to endear his work to generations of Victorians and make him the mouthpiece of his age.

Meanwhile, whatever they thought of his poetry, his friends were fascinated by the man: the tall, powerful frame, massive hands, dark complexion, straggling locks, a majestic nose, large, brooding eyes, a deep voice that seemed to emanate from some internal cavern, and a social manner breathtakingly naïve and spontaneous. He was utterly careless in his dress, drank a good deal of port and only felt at ease when lost in a cloud of tobacco smoke. Very much of a recluse, a tremendous egotist obviously, yet shy, painfully blunt at times (but with no conscious desire to offend), and seemingly incapable of saying anything, even "How-do-you-do?", except when he really meant it. Most disconcerting. His moods could be troublesome, too. He was inclined to be gloomy—"the black blood of the Tennysons", he would say—and then would suddenly light up and become all fire and eloquence. For people accustomed to wearing the mask of convention, here was a phenomenon: a man all of one piece, who felt and spoke from greater depths than ordinary men, in whom a channel seemed to run, clear and swift, from some source that they could only surmise. They called it genius.

The Tennysons, with their eldest child Hallam, came to the Isle of Wight in 1853, the poet in need of a permanent home and seclusion. At Farringford, at the foot of the high down, about two miles from Freshwater church and a mile from the bay, they found the ideal house, late Georgian, of yellow brick, not pretty, but with a lovely view from the big drawing-room window over sloping fields dotted with elms towards the ever-changing sea. There was a small park, a larger farm, plenty of greenery to hide the poet from the world and a riot of unspoiled nature where he could walk with his long, clumping stride, eagerly drawing inspiration from the flight of birds, the wild flowers on the downs, the movement of the sea.

Soon the tall figure in his broad-brimmed sombrero and flapping cloak became a familiar sight in the neighbourhood. From the tree-enshrouded house, crammed with antiques, plaster casts from Michelangelo, prints, photographs, books, with red walls and a wealth of crimson plush, he would emerge after a day spent rolling the lawn or cutting glades through the copses to pace, muttering to himself, over the downs or through the lanes of Freshwater. A small boy told the

Farringford (overleaf)
St. Agnes Church, Freshwater Bay (overleaf)
Compton Bay

village postman that he had met Tennyson making poems for the Queen under the stars. Fishermen reported that he went with them sometimes at night and recited wonderful words to them while they rowed. Old men of the village were liable to become involved in earnest discussions on God and the immortality of the soul. All this was strange, but the poet, viewed with awe at first, soon endeared himself. He was charming with children and never tired of talking to simple people about their lives and hopes. The coastguards, the shepherds, the farm workers, all got to know him, and their respect did not spring from the fact that Prince Albert himself had called on the Tennysons while they were settling in. Many of them read and loved his poetry, the little purple volume of *In Memoriam* particularly, which had found its way into tens of thousands of homes throughout the land.

Behind the massive front door of his home invited visitors from the mainland, having survived the tedious journey by cart over unmade tracks from Yarmouth, found Tennyson relaxed and genial. Coventry Patmore, Jowett and F. D. Maurice, the last two at the centre of contemporary religious strife, heralded the flood of famous people who for the next forty years talked, argued, sang, played, geologized and botanized with the "Jupiter of Farringford" or merely worshipped at his shrine. Anne Thackeray, daughter of the novelist, declared in amazement: "Everybody at Freshwater is either a genius, or a poet, or a painter or peculiar in some way." In the intervals of composing, which he did in clouds of tobacco smoke in his small, top-floor study or later in a summer-house which he had built in the grounds, Tennyson became one of the intellectual centres of Victorian England, discussing Irish Home Rule, or the future of the Empire or the extension of the franchise with Gladstone, metaphysics with churchmen, astronomy with Sir John Herschel, geology with Darwin. But his life-blood was poetry and ever since as a child of five he had chanted his first meaningless but intoxicating line—"With slaughterous sons of thunder rolled the flood"—the technique of verse, its subtleties, its form had obsessed him, the sound and rhythm of words had filled his mind. Everything at Farringford revolved round the work in progress, the work planned or the work completed.

The climax of the day would be reached when an audience keyed to the highest pitch of expectation gathered in the big drawing-room to hear him recite. Passages from "Maud" would sweep over them in a voice alternately powerful, soothing, dramatic, filled to breaking point with quivering pathos. Sometimes tears ran down his cheeks like rain. Verses from his "King Arthur" sounded like "harmonious thunder and lightning"—it was enough, wrote Edward Lear, to "make you stand on your head". His listeners wept, too, and the emotional scenes became so distressing that before reading "Enoch Arden" he had to beg them not to go into hysterics. The best description of Tennyson reading was given by Anne Thackeray: "It is a sort of mystical incantation, a chant in which every note rises and falls and reverberates again. As we sit round the twilit room at Farringford, with its great oriel window looking to the garden, across fields of hyacinths and self-sowed daffodils, looking towards the sea, we seem to be carried by a tide not unlike the ocean's sound; it fills the room, it ebbs and flows away; and when we leave, it is with a strange music in our ears, feeling that we have, for the first time, perhaps, heard what we may have read a hundred times before."

But the explanation of Tennyson's spell lay not only in his personality. His poetry suited exactly the Victorian mood. A high morality, love of God and beauty, spoke in every line. It was tender, noble, and never shocking. In strife-ridden times it breathed reassurance, teaching that Man is in the hand of God and will pass through this vale of tears towards an immortal destiny. It preached duty, faith, love and hope. "On leaving Tennyson," wrote the French critic Taine, "we can listen, in the same spirit, to the grave voice of the master of the house who is saying evening prayers before the kneeling servants."

And yet, though Tennyson achieved a fame never enjoyed by any other poet in his lifetime he remained morbidly sensitive and unsure of himself. Poetry enabled him to buy Farringford. The first edition of "Enoch Arden", with a printing of 60,000, made him £6,000 in one year. Continually he was confronted with adulation amounting to worship. But criticism, even from ignorant schoolboys, could distress him for days, and even late in life a letter from an anonymous carper made him exclaim that he wished he had never written a line. As for celebrity-hunters, he abhorred them. He had a terror of prying eyes which sprang perhaps from experiences early in life when his father, the rector of Somersby in Lincolnshire, had been the target of local scandal-mongers. Tennyson had gone to Farringford to escape the mob, but the mob followed him. "Most people who visit Freshwater ask for the house of the poet," blithely stated a contemporary guide-book, and indeed they did. Admirers shinned up trees overlooking the house, they climbed banks, bolder spirits marched up the drive and rang the front door bell. Glancing towards the window at lunch one day, he caught sight of a nose flattened against a pane, its owner in process of observing to invisible friends: "You can see him well from here!"

One and all, if caught, got short shrift. There is a story of an American family, poor but devoted to the bard. Their one ambition was to cast eyes on him and if possible exchange a few words. So they saved and scraped and at last had enough money to pay for the Atlantic crossing, the journey by train to Brockenhurst, the onward trip by horse-bus to Lymington, the ferry, the cart over unmade tracks to Freshwater. In due course, pale but triumphant, they arrived at the gate of Farringford—and there, pacing the drive in the famous sombrero and cloak, was none other than the poet himself. The father of the family took a pace forward, spoke: "Sirr——" But Tennyson raised an admonishing hand and deep from the cavernous chest came the words: "*This may not be!*" Disconsolately the family took one last adoring look at the sombre figure, turned, and went back by the next boat to America.

But suspicious of strangers to the extent that he once fled from a flock of sheep, mistaking them for admirers, Tennyson was never arrogant and the greatest tribute to his character is that, despite worldwide fame, he remained simple and unaffected. Few men have possessed his gift for making lifelong friends. Freshwater in summer positively hummed with life and gaiety, all centred on the poet. There would be long walks to Alum Bay or eastwards past Compton with Browning or Edward Fitzgerald; romps on the garden with Hallam, his second son Lionel and a host of other children; dinner parties lasting for hours where wit and humour flowed; and many people, such was his hold over contemporaries, believed they were present at the making of history when they saw him descend at lunch-time from his study where he was working on "The Idylls of the King".

In the middle years at Farringford a phenomenal woman appeared on the scene who was to gain her own modicum of immortality, Mrs. Julia Cameron, the photographer. Faded examples of her work can still be picked up occasionally in island antique shops or at auctions, mostly portraits of eminent Victorians, slightly out of focus, but full of atmosphere and personality. Some of them are masterpieces, far surpassing other work done in her time and in professional circles the ebullient, kind-hearted and eccentric Mrs. Cameron is still much respected as a pioneer who, with the most primitive equipment, produced pictures which some modern photographers might envy. Down the road from Farringford towards Freshwater Bay you can see her tall, sharp-gabled house "Dimbola" where she came to live in 1860. Her desire was to be close to her friend Tennyson, for whom she had conceived a passionate regard.

In that year, accordingly, the plain, plump, energetic woman, swathed in trailing robes of gorgeous colour, towing six children, some orphaned nieces and a husband twenty years older than herself, descended on Freshwater. She had been born in India: father a Scotsman, mother an aristocratic French emigrée. Her husband had helped to codify the Indian laws and was a jurist of note. Mrs. Cameron had not yet discovered photography; instead, she flung the whole of her florid personality into worshipping the bard, doing kindnesses to the local people and smothering the Tennysons with gifts. She was tiresome but lovable and under her assault the bastions of Farringford fell. She brought legs of mutton to the door, sent a pair of loose Eastern trousers in purple and gold for the poet, followed by two Japanese teacups, a hot-water bottle and a teapot. The gifts expressed overflowing goodwill; it hardly mattered what they were. When the Farringford piano was out of order she sent eight men sweating across the fields with her own. The children's birthdays brought more gifts —not always to the right child. With Tennyson she was soon on "Alfred" and "Julia" terms, a privilege which she captured and waved like a banner. She begged manuscripts from him, bossed him about and at night sometimes summoned him to go down with her to the beach to admire the raging sea.

Then someone gave her a camera, two large boxes, one sliding inside the other, and she flung herself into photography. From now on, she, too, would create. Her aim was artistry—none of the *carte de visite* kind of pictures so popular at the time with their stereotyped poses and dead-pan expressions. She would catch the souls of her subjects, whether they liked it or not, however long it took and whatever the exertions involved. These were considerable. Her camera had a colossus of a lens and used huge plates measuring 12 inches by 15, requiring an exposure lasting from three to seven minutes. They were prepared by what was known as the wet collodion process in which the fluid had to be poured evenly over them before they were sensitized in a silver nitrate bath and inserted, still wet, in the camera. After the exposure came fixing, washing, drying, then heating and varnishing. The varnish often cracked the plate and it was necessary to start all over again. Washing entailed floods of water which had to be drawn from a well. And sitters, of course, could not turn themselves into marble all that easily and were bound to move.

Nothing daunted, Mrs. Cameron converted her coal-house into a dark-room, a glazed chicken-shed into a studio, and started looking for sitters throughout the byways and highways of the island. If she took to a face it was useless for man, woman or child to protest. "I am Mrs. Cameron," she would say. "You may have heard of me. I would like to take your photograph. Will you allow me to do so?" The question was rhetorical. From plough or kitchen the victim would be hauled off to the fowl-house, dumped into a chair and, holding maybe an egg-cup and the gardener's scythe to represent Father Time, be bullied into enduring seven whole minutes—or seven times seven —of static hell. Famous people who came to Farringford were never secure. Tennyson, of course, was one of her earliest sitters, and when Longfellow stayed, a session had to be booked with the camera. "You will have to do just what she says," said Tennyson, leading him to the slaughter. "I will come back soon and see what is left of you." Garibaldi on his visit in 1864 was astonished to see a plump woman, her hands stained with chemicals, kneeling to him in the drive. He thought she was a beggar, but still said no when told it was Mrs. Cameron imploring him to sit for his photograph.

But Tennyson admired her work and in a weak moment, because the camera was never meant to tell a story, asked her to illustrate "The Idylls of the King". Immortality beckoned and Mrs. Cameron pounced on her new task. Properties were procured: boats, hollow tree-stumps, yards of gauze to represent the sea, armour, weapons and an ocean of flowers. Then the search for characters began. The porter at Yarmouth pier was cast for King Arthur—and was pronounced a great success. A young summer visitor was captured as Guinevere, and to illustrate the lines, "And while she grovelled at his feet she felt the King's breath wander o'er her neck", was obliged to lie on the floor for two hours clutching the porter's ankle. Mr. Cameron, when not overcome with giggles, performed nobly as Merlin in the tree-stump. But Launcelot proved hard to find. Mrs. Cameron wrote to friends: "Do you know of a Launcelot?" She even thought of advertising. Finally she found him in the Bishop of Salford standing in the firelight at a tea-party. In ringing tones she announced her discovery to Tennyson who, too short-sighted to see the man clearly, boomed in reply: "I want a face well worn with human passion!" The bishop, fortunately, saw the joke.

The illustration of the "Idylls" saw the lawn at Dimbola littered with developing frames, dishes of collodion and groups of bearded men and wimpled women recovering from their sittings in the hen-house, Mrs. Cameron's husky and imperious voice dominating them all. But the work did not exhaust her. Balls, dinner parties and theatricals filled the evenings.

While Tennyson was hard at work at Farringford, G. F. Watts was painting in a house given to him on the road to Alum Bay. Visitors basked in the atmosphere of intellect and imagination as though Fresh-water was a second Athens. Occasionally the poet would be invited to Osborne, whence he would return with incoherent accounts of talks with the Queen, so moved he had been to see her in her widow's weeds on her lonely pinnacle. Jenny Lind, the Swedish Nightingale, sang at Farringford, Arthur Sullivan played, and there were mementoes of a notable visit in a previous year when Queen Emma of the Sandwich Islands had arrived with a dusky suite and been installed on a throne made from an ilex tree felled on the estate. Farringford itself now had a ballroom where huge tea-parties were given and dances at which Tennyson himself would waltz, after walking perhaps fifteen miles during the day, before returning with port and pipe to his study.

Then, as suddenly as she had arrived, Mrs. Cameron left with her patriarchal husband for Ceylon, taking a cow with her to provide milk on the voyage and tipping porters at Southampton with signed copies of her photographs. Tennyson now had another house near Haslemere, but several months each year were still spent at Farringford, where the social life continued unabated and the contrast grew ever wider between the ageing poet with his simple tastes, his love of soli-tude and the demands made on him by a world of admirers. Privacy became practically impossible; his daily walks on the downs took the form of a procession in which young and old, friends and total strangers tagged on as a chattering group behind the sombre, gypsy-like figure.

It was pathetic, noted an acquaintance, that his life should be spent in a blaze of publicity when he was happiest with books, flowers and one or two intimate friends.

But Tennyson plodded on through the years, amazingly unaffected by the surrounding din, carrying his inner climate with him, gruff, earnest, always unpredictable and always, deep in his mind, revolving the eternal problems of human destiny and the meaning of life whose beauties and horrors he saw with agonizing clarity. The death of his beloved friend Arthur Hallam, though it had happened half a century ago, was a wound which never healed. It nourished questions which he came to see could not be answered in this world. Was life meaningless, nothing but "a murmur of gnats in the gloom, or a moment's anger of bees in their hive?" Was death the end, or was the spirit world, which he sensed like "a great ocean pressing round us on every side", the true reality? He questioned friends about their beliefs. When a girl, young enough to be his granddaughter, said she was sure the spirit survived, he replied with grave humility: "Yes, I too hold it so. I have tried to say it—to show it—that the body is the husk, the shell. But at times these new lights, this science wearies and perplexes me ..." Certainty eluded him to the end; religious dogma had never been a comfort. In some moods he could cling to no more than the barest thread of conviction that "there is something which watches over us". It was these conflicts of hope and doubt, never quite submerging the small voice of faith and the promptings of his genius, which made him so human.

While criticizing Tennyson for the airiness of his metaphysics, the indefiniteness of his knowledge, the looseness of his political reasoning, Lord Acton was one of those who detected the bedrock of his personality as a grave groping for religious certainty, and his brooding eyes, the deep lines that ran from nose to mouth conveyed a sense of power in perplexity familiar to all who knew him. But it is the small recorded incidents which seem to bring him alive: peering through his steel-rimmed spectacles at wild flowers on the downs; walking with his American publisher through the moonlit park at Farringford when he suddenly fell on his knees and cried out: "Violets, man, violets! Smell them and you'll sleep the better"; the night when he came downstairs in the early hours to give a whole chicken to his new dog because he feared the animal might be lonely.

It was as an old man in his eighty-first year, in October 1889, that, on the short trip from Lymington to Yarmouth, he composed "Crossing the Bar". The poem came to him in a moment and he jotted it down on the inside of an old envelope. When he got back to Farringford he went to his study and wrote out a fair copy. Earlier in that year he had been seriously ill with rheumatic gout, and as he slowly recovered the nurse tending him had found him a difficult patient. She had scolded him and said that instead of grumbling he ought to write a hymn in gratitude for being restored to health. Now, as she came into the study, she found him sitting at his desk with a paper before him. He handed it to her and said simply: "Will this do for you, old woman?" But when she read the poem it came as a great shock and without a word she turned and ran from the room: it seemed to her that he had written his own death-song. That night he showed the lines to his eldest son Hallam, who said: "That is the crown of your life's work."

> *Sunset and evening star,*
> *And one clear call for me!*
> *And may there be no moaning of the bar*
> *When I put out to sea.*
>
> *But such a tide as moving seems asleep,*
> *Too full for sound and foam,*
> *When that which drew from out the boundless deep*
> *Turns again home . . .*

To me, these are the most moving lines in the poem, particularly the last one, with the inexorable *turns*, and the power and longing that lie behind it. Those three strong beats—*turns again home*—seem to sum up the whole of Tennyson's spiritual striving, a lifetime given up to a search which never ended, which racked him with doubt, and left him, except in moments of poetic intuition, uncertain to the end.

He died three years after writing this poem, not at Farringford, but at his other home in Sussex, with the moonlight streaming in through the window, clasping his Shakespeare, and was buried in Westminster Abbey, mourned by the whole of Victorian England. At Farringford, now an hotel, the only visible mementoes left are some of his books and furniture, and the green gate by which he left the garden for the downs. But his memory is still much alive among the people of Freshwater. He is their poet. He immortalized the beauties of their scenery. And for nearly forty years he made this corner of the island a place of pilgrimage for the highest to the lowest in the land. Finally, I must confess that when I stay at Farringford I still seem to sense his presence, or rather I conjure it, in the house which today is still as someone described it in the year of his death, "remote as though the jar of the outside world had never entered it", and in the garden where the sea-roar comes up from Freshwater Bay, just as he heard it, sensing in those sounds the pulse and rhythm of eternity.

V

WRECKS AND SMUGGLING

On the East side of Freshwater Bay the road to Ventnor rears steeply over Afton Down and then performs a gentle switchback before dropping to the long straight ride, only a quarter of a mile from the sea, to Chale. For ten miles you are almost alone with the wooded hills stretching inland and the bare ploughed fields skirting the low cliffs by the shore. The only buildings are farms scattered here and there in the valleys or on the slopes. Behind you, as you drive, the great sweep of the bay on this south-west side of the island is unfolding, very open, very impressive, with the curve of the shore and the skyward slant of the cliffs, the sea rolling in long parallel lines of breakers and the thin thread of beach arching round till it vanishes below Tennyson Down.

Here you sniff the sharp air of freedom and pictures from past history rise in the mind. A row of cottages strung out on the seaward side at the head of a chine is all you can see from this road of Brook. The village, no more than a few scattered houses, lies inland behind trees. But here to the manor house in 1499 came Henry VII when inspecting the island defences, and was so pleased with his reception that he presented the lady of the manor with his drinking horn and granted her a fat buck yearly from the forest of Parkhurst for life, and here, on a cold spring day of 1864, Garibaldi came to stay with a local family on his triumphant visit to England after the success of his Italian campaign. Three days later, looking very grand in a white poncho lined with red, an embroidered red shirt and coloured tie, he went to Farringford, the villagers waited for two hours outside the gate to see him, and genially, at the Tennysons' request, he planted a tree on the front lawn, shielded from a sharp east wind and the eyes of the vulgar by a canvas screen lined with pages from *Punch*. Tennyson, envious perhaps of the man of action, gave him some political advice, opining afterwards that in worldly matters Garibaldi seemed to have the "divine stupidity of a hero", and the hero, after patting the Tennyson children on the head, drove off to the ragged cheers of the bystanders.

But Brook summons another picture, more grim and powerful. After you pass those cottages above the shore the surface of the road changes and the tyres take up a high-pitched hum, like the wind in a ship's rigging. The scenery becomes more desolate, with gaunt trees slanting away from the prevailing wind; loneliness broods over the fields and downs. In winter-time, when like as not a stiff breeze will be blowing inshore and the waves out of sight below will be roaring in tight regiments of surf, the innumerable tales of wreck and disaster on this coast come to mind, ships in their hundreds that wind and tide carried helpless on to the dangerous Atherfield Ledge, that stretch back, ghost-like, through the centuries, and whose names, even, only begin to emerge from obscurity in the time of George III. Then one thinks of this desolate shore, the handful of farmers and fishermen secure from the storm in their cottages until the gun at Brook or Brighstone boomed and the lifeboat crews dropped their daily tasks and raced for the boathouse. One can imagine, too, the sweating, groaning task of launching the boat in days before the invention of tractors. Cart horses had to be fetched from the nearest farms and harnessed to the heavy carriage, then the boat was dragged slowly down over shingle and sand to the breakers. As far as they could go the horses were led into the water until, judging the moment, the coxwain shouted "Launch!", helpers hauled on ropes, the boat slid forward, the crew struck their oars deep into the water, and with luck and a strong pull she would be afloat.

But wrecks along these shores are centuries older than lifeboats and there was no rescue service at all until after fifteen lives had been lost from one ship in 1859 when the local fishermen in their frail craft had been unable to reach her. Then boats were established at Brook and two miles to the east at Brighstone, since when the island lifeboats as a whole have saved well over a thousand lives.

The praises of lifeboat crews have often been sung, but only a particular case can bring home the perils which these men faced voluntarily at all times of the year, at any hour of the day or night, or the agonies of suspense which their womenfolk endured when, as often happened because of the sparse population, every able-bodied man in the family crammed on his oilskins and risked the hazards of the storm.

Among the twenty serious wrecks which occurred in the fifty years up to 1933, the loss of the *Sirenia* will long be remembered and the drama has been recorded by more than one writer. On foggy days without a breath of wind it is a peculiarity of the south coast that the seas off Atherfield, which lies between Brighstone and Chale, are often full of sound and fury. So it was on the morning of 9th March, 1888. In the distance the waves could be heard striking the outer ledges at intervals with a hollow roar. Later on, as the tide came in, the roar became a continuous roll, with great breakers crashing on the shore. It was one of those days when everyone in Brighstone thought of the lifeboat and wondered anxiously: would there be a call? Down on the shore, a mile to the eastward at Whale Chine, despite the fog and high seas a gang was working on the wreck of a ship that had been stranded there fourteen months before. In the village a member of the lifeboat crew was building a barn. All these men, in their several ways, reacted quickly to the disaster which followed.

At about three in the afternoon, when the fog was thinning slightly, the full-rigged ship *Sirenia* of 1,590 tons, bound from San Francisco to Dunkirk, impaled herself on the rocks at Atherfield Ledge, about a mile from shore. Though unaware at first that his ship was already lost, the captain, who had his wife, three children and a crew of twenty-six on board, started blowing blasts on the siren. These were heard by the coastguard at Atherfield who immediately sent word to the coxswain of the lifeboat and by one of the men working on the wreck. He looked up and saw what at first he took to be a rain-cloud; a second glance told him that it was a cloud of canvas, for the *Sirenia* had been under full sail when she struck. Quickly he ran up the cliffs to tell his father, a member of the Brighstone crew, and found him at home. Taking a quick bite of bread and cheese, the older man dropped everything, ran to the carter to tell him his horses would be needed, then down to the lifeboat house. Soon after, the gun boomed, summoning the rest of the crew. When they arrived, including the man who had been building the barn, they thought they had never seen such gigantic seas.

By now it was well after four o'clock and, with the fog still persisting, it was beginning to get dark. Into the raging sea, by the light of flickering candle-lamps, the boat with its crew of ten plus the coxswain, his assistant and the bowman, was launched. After a hard pull they got under the lee of the *Sirenia* and took off the captain's wife, his children, their nurse and an apprentice—these for the first trip. To land more at high tide with heavy seas pounding the beach was thought to be impossible. So the boat, the *Worcester Cadet*, was rowed back across the mile of boiling water and several times the coxswain had to turn her head to meet the waves or else she would have been swamped. The first survivors were landed and it was intended to return to the *Sirenia* at low water when there would be less sea on the beach and greater numbers could be put ashore. But now it began to blow, at first a few gusts and then a strong south-west gale. This meant that the seas by the ledge would soon be wilder than ever.

It was impossible to wait; there was no time to be lost. The heavy boat was dragged back on to the carriage, the carriage was turned round, and in pitch-darkness now the *Worcester Cadet* headed back for the second time to the *Sirenia*. Rowing through the breakers was a dangerous business; once out of them it was possible to set a sail. But close to the wreck a very heavy sea was running and after a grapnel had been successfully thrown from the lifeboat, the rescuers, as they came alongside, at one moment found themselves level with the *Sirenia*'s rail, and at the next, twenty feet below it. Oars were smashed and several times the boat struck heavily against the ship's side. But jumping or sliding down a rope, thirteen of the *Sirenia*'s crew managed to get aboard. Then the order was given to cast off. This had to be done quickly, but the axe normally carried in the life-boat had been washed overboard and before the bowman could hack through the rope with his knife a mountainous sea, black tipped with white, came surging up astern. The bow reared crazily and the thirteen men fell backwards in a heap, throwing the coxswain and his assistant out of the boat. Then she broke loose, the sea took charge and she began to drive helplessly towards the shore. A few seconds later, another huge wave struck her and in one fatal corkscrew motion the boat, with a total of twenty-two men in their boots and heavy oilskins still aboard, turned turtle. Then she righted herself, and miraculously most of the men managed to clamber back and find their oars. Then they looked round for their coxswain and his assistant. When they saw they had gone there was only one thought: row back to find them. So in the dark and the howling storm the men, drenched and many of them injured, turned back and rowed astern of the *Sirenia*, shouted and burnt flares—all in vain. Their brave coxswain and his friend had gone, and so had two of the survivors from the *Sirenia*.

That was not the end of the story. The boat then turned for the shore. The rescued men were landed, fresh volunteers replaced exhausted or injured members of the crew, and preparations were made for a third sortie. For the third time the boat was dragged on to the carriage, the carriage was turned, the boat was launched—and by now a cheerless dawn was breaking. Meanwhile, the Brook lifeboat had also put out, crossing five miles in a boiling cauldron to reach the wreck. It was almost there when it, too, was nearly engulfed by a huge sea and three men were swept overboard. Two clambered back and the boat was turned to search for the third; his cries for help could still be heard over the greying waters. But the search was in vain, though the captain of the *Sirenia* refused further assistance so that it could continue, and by the time it was broken off the boat had been pounded and smothered by the breakers at Atherfield Ledge and every man in the crew was exhausted. So they anchored, shivering with cold, without food or water, intending to ride out the night and go back to the wreck at dawn. But when dawn came they were more dead than alive, and though they struggled to reach the *Sirenia* they were forced to give up and, hoisting a sail, beat back to their station. By then, the *Worcester Cadet* had made her third trip and rescued the remainder from the *Sirenia*. Result: thirty people had been saved and three men from the lifeboats had lost their lives. Can it be wondered that in Brighstone and Brook they still speak with pride of that night long ago?

But besides the saving of lives the word "wreck" has other suggestions for the islanders in the shape of free gifts from the sea of food, clothing, timber and the thousand things that a well-fitted ship contains. This has always been so, and in the past, when fishermen and farm labourers supported large families on a few shillings a week, who can blame them for grabbing casks of butter or anything that eased their lot? They were not the only people who saw the potentialities of wrecks, either. If one studies an old map of the south-east corner of the island between St. Catherine's Point and Dunnose it is extraordinary to find that in bygone days no less than five parishes had frontages along these five miles of coast, each stretching back inland in a strip like a slice of cake—and this regardless of parishioners' convenience. The people of Ventnor and neighbourhood, for instance, had to trudge over five miles northwards to worship or bury their dead at Newchurch. Further west, they had to scramble over high and almost trackless downs to Godshill, with the result that in winter some funeral processions proved lethal to the mourners. All this because in those days parish boundaries coincided with the boundaries of manors and since the time of Edward I lords of the manor had established their right to "wreck of the sea". Each, therefore, wanted a strip of sea-coast in his domain, however short, however unpromising, as the receiving end of the ocean's cornucopia.

In days of atrocious or non-existent roads the disposal of wrecks and their cargoes on the spot was the only practicable course, but the arrangement was open to terrible abuse. What was a wreck? If a ship was temporarily stranded and got off again at high tide, presumably she was not, even if help was needed to refloat her. If survivors came ashore, presumably they were still responsible for the ship and her cargo. Only when a ship was a total wreck and there were no survivors had the lord of the manor an indisputable right to everything in her down to the last nail, the last square inch of canvas. Therefore there was a temptation to withhold assistance, particularly in days when life was cheap and the fishermen themselves along this coast often succumbed to the perils of the sea. There are travellers' tales, some dating from the mid-eighteenth century, reporting that "country people of the meaner sort" were over-zealous in looting wrecks and were more intent on plundering than giving help. But as for deliberate wrecking by hanging out false lights, there is no evidence at all, except for a story that on stormy nights the inhabitants would tie up the leg of an old horse and drive it along the cliffs with a lantern fixed to its head to imitate the movement of a ship's light. This is obviously nonsense and I should think that for centuries the attitude of the people here has been the same roughly as it is today: they did all that courage and skill could achieve to help ships in distress and save the lives of their crews. But if a fat freighter did come ashore and nothing could be done to save her, they were well organized to rob the lord of the manor of his due (and in modern times the Receiver of Wrecks!) and they looked on it as a joyful occasion. As the ship was carried inshore beyond the point of no return a great shout would go up from the cliffs: "She's ours, boys!" and the men would wait to see what Davy Jones's Bounty had brought them.

Winkle Street

This attitude of "help where we can, otherwise let's help ourselves" seems to me full of good sense and in a book written between the wars an islander who himself served in the lifeboats and paid tribute to their work wrote quite naturally of a "most marvellous wreck" which occurred in 1902 because of the good things which were cast up—bloaters, lard, butter, sausage, pork and casks of spirits which the locals drained into any receptacle they could lay hands on, including their mouths, until they were lying about dead-drunk on the shore. On another occasion, in 1910, a fishing vessel ran right up to the beach near Walpan Chine, disgorging delectable fish and also baskets to carry them in—very obliging. Helpful, too, in time of strict rationing, was a massive consignment of bacon, pork and lard washed up in Freshwater Bay during the First World War. The stuff could either be sold or consumed, and if coastguards and police were too vigilant the local fishermen could still earn good money from wrecks by helping to salvage the cargo.

Radar now keeps these gifts well out to sea and if people at the Back of the Wight are called lawless today it can only be in the special and to them hair-splitting sense that they fail to distinguish between jetsam of known ownership and treasure-trove. If something gets washed up from a ship whose owners are alive and kicking then you are not legally entitled to help yourself, as it still belongs to them whether it lies between high and low water or anywhere else. But if, on your morning walk in Chale Bay, you should come across a Piece of Eight then the loot is yours. The possibility of finding such treasure-trove is small, but it exists. The coins may well be there, but they are hard to find. An islander showed me a bagful of Pieces of Eight, twelve or fourteen of them, which he had picked up at a place appropriately called the Money Hole, and a gold Pistole and a Real bearing the lions of León and the castles of Castile, all minted in Lima and dated, according to experts, about 1700. In case you want to go hunting for them, Pieces of Eight have the shape of an irregular oblong, about two inches long by an inch broad and weigh from two to three ounces. On one side is a double cross, like the cross of Lorraine, and on the other there may be a faint tracing which looks like the figure 8. They are solid silver, of course, but rust to a dark chocolate colour so that, even when found, they are hard to recognize. But in the last century it is said that people picked up these "dollars" by the handful at Blackgang, and they are thought to come from a Spanish

81

treasure ship wrecked off the coast as it was being towed to Portsmouth after capture in Vigo Bay in 1702. There is even a tale of a man finding ingots of silver and simply hacking off lumps for sale in Newport when he was in need of money. But, alas, that was long ago.

After you have travelled seven miles through an empty landscape along this coast road from Brook, it is a relief to come across human habitations again at Chale. Lying at the foot of St. Catherine's Down (773 feet), this, though, is one of the less attractive of the island villages with its slate-roofed cottages built of stone, its gloomy church and churchyard and the tall Perpendicular tower lowering over the surrounding fields. For countless mariners in the past Chale spelt disaster. In the desolate bay and along this coast sixty ships were wrecked in just over sixty years, fourteen of them on one night in 1757. In all the island parishes the right of wreck was combined with the duty of burying corpses washed ashore and along the north wall of the churchyard, whose box tombs are said to have been used by smugglers to conceal their loot, are ranged the graves of men and women drowned in 1836, when in a few minutes the full-rigged ship *Clarendon* was smashed to pieces on the rocks with heavy loss of life.

Up to that time, when steps were at last taken to build an adequate lighthouse near the shore at St. Catherine's Point, the only warning to mariners had been a feeble gleam winking through the mists from the top of the down, and for over two hundred years, since the dissolution of the monasteries, there had been no light at all. The islanders will show you, though, a curious octagonal tower, obviously very ancient, standing on what used to be called Chale Mountain. There, from 1314 to the time of Henry VIII, a priest was maintained to say masses for the souls of the drowned and burn a warning light, a pious exercise paid for in perpetuity by one Walter de Godeton, who had leased the manor of Chale. In 1314 he had been involved in serious trouble. A French ship carrying casks of white wine broke up on Atherfield Ledge, and though the master and some of the crew reached safety local fishermen seized part of the cargo and sold it to de Godeton. The master of the ship then claimed that the wine was his and in due course the court at Winchester ordered the temporary lord of the manor to reimburse him. This should have been the end of the matter. But unfortunately the wine belonged to a religious community, the monastery of Livers in Picardy, and a further charge of sacrilege was raised against the luckless Walter, reinforced, it is said, by fulminations from the Pope. As a result, the sinner was ordered to build a lighthouse on the down overlooking the scene of the wreck and to pay for a priest to tend it. So Walter paid, but undoubtedly it was the priest and his successors who suffered, shivering in lonely majesty on this wind-swept down. The tower has been called the most interesting relic in all England of practical medieval piety.

Neither Chale nor Niton, a larger village two miles further on behind the Undercliff, are much frequented by visitors, but scraps of information have come down to us which suggest that Niton may have had some importance in ancient times. An intriguing story can be traced back to the Sicilian writer Diodorus Siculus who recorded in 25 B.C. that at low tide the Ancient Britons used to take their tin in carts to an island called "Icta" for transport to France. This trade is said to have been carried on right into Roman times. Where was Icta? Could it have been the Isle of Wight? Remembering that the Solent was said to have been fordable at one time, some authorities say yes, others are doubtful. But to support their view the former produce plausible evidence. Tin was much in demand, of course, in the Bronze Age. The Phoenicians fetched it from Cornwall and so did the Greeks. To cut out their competitors the Greeks opened up a land route through Marseilles and this route seems to have led along the English coast to the Isle of Wight, as being the most direct line from Cornwall to the final destination. The evidence? Tradition has it that there was an ancient British road from Cornwall to Leap in Hampshire and along it occur significant place-names: Stansa Bay, Stans Ore Point, derived from the Latin *stannum*, meaning tin. Finally, beside this road Greek and Roman coins have been found, and at Gurnard, the nearest point on the island to Leap, there was formerly a Roman building which has long since fallen into the sea. In the island, too, further suggestive evidence comes to light. Southwards from Gurnard there was once a straight road leading towards modern Newport called Rue Street and off this road was Gonneville Lane. Rue and Gonneville are place-names on the Somme which might have been the receiving point for the tin. In the island, Niton is on the direct line from Gurnard and close to Niton is Puckaster Cove, a name derived from the Latin, and though today no longer able to embark a mouse, obviously a port in Roman times. Finally, we find that a farm near Puckaster was called Buddle, and a buddle is a large frame of boards used to wash metalliferous ore. All of which is suggestive, to say the least. But there is one further supporting fact: the Cornish tin trade was continued right into the fifteenth century and Southampton was then its mart.

So in prehistoric times sleepy Niton may have been a busy place and centuries later it was busy again—in the smuggling trade, which had its heyday in the hundred years from 1750. But it would be wrong, apparently, to imagine that a smugglers' village was a scene of constant revelry. In 1801, one visitor at least found Niton very prim and proper. There were three hundred inhabitants living in fifty-two cottages, each with its garden, its pig and its orchard. To earn a livelihood it seemed that the men either fished or worked on the land, renting their cottages from one of the local farmers and paying the rent with their wages in the harvest month. This meant that there was not much money to spare. Yet their wives never went to work, their children looked neat and well cared for, and there were no paupers in the village. What was the secret? They kept it to themselves. One thing was noticeable about them: they were very suspicious of strangers. But perhaps this was because their life, as in other island villages, was completely self-contained and they rarely saw a strange face. There was no road to Newport in those days and parish registers show that for a hundred and fifty years family names common in one village in the area seldom occurred in another.

On the other hand, we know they had a secret, and the secret was brandy. In 1860, when smuggling was in fact on the wane, the poet Sidney Dobell stayed near Niton and wrote: "The strange, wild, lawless life of the solemn, lawful-seeming people is an inexhaustible study. The whole population are smugglers. Everybody has an ostensible occupation, but nobody gets his money by it or cares to work in it. Here are fishermen who never fish, but always have pockets full of money, and farmers whose farming consists in ploughing the deep by night, and whose daily time is spent in standing like herons on lookout posts. Nearly the whole village lives in masquerade, even to the names of the villagers. Hardly a man is known by his lawful surname, and we had been here weeks before I suspected that the nomenclature in use was no more real than a play. Everything suggests the abnormal sort of bandit or clan life of the place. Here we are on a desolate shore, but living safely in a house which has not even on its ground floor a single shutter, and where the front door is often unlocked all night, with a certainty against molestation."

Smugglers, it seems, had no time for petty thieving; the rewards from "free trade" were too great. Every village had a chosen leader who organized the business on a co-operative basis and the names of the more successful became legendary after their death: Ralph Stone of Niton, for instance, described as a quiet but fearless operator, who by day dressed—only dressed!—as a local farmer in velveteen shooting coat and waistcoat, white hat, fancy trousers and Wellington boots. Such men were the kings of the village. To the cost of the liquor and the expense of running it over, usually from Cherbourg, the villagers subscribed so much in return for a share in the booty. The outward trip, often in six-oared rowboats or in sailing ships of up to forty tons, was usually uneventful because the smugglers could choose their own time of leaving, and if they were intercepted they could pose as harmless fishermen and there would be nothing to prove that they were not. All the same, there were not many men today who would contemplate rowing over to Cherbourg and back with much enthusiasm. The return journey, however, was quite a different matter. Infinite precautions were taken by the smugglers to conceal their cargo of "tubs", to arrange liaison with the shore to make certain of a clear run-in and quick disposal of the stuff when it was landed. And this was not only to avoid the financial loss of a confiscated cargo; the smaller fry stood to serve a year in the notorious Fleet prison if they were caught and the ringleaders five years in a man-of-war.

So we hear of many devices to ensure safe arrival: false bottoms to boats to conceal the tubs, wooden troughs under the ballast of sailing ships for the same purpose, and—supreme impertinence!—when tobacco was being run the contraband was sometimes spun into imitation tarred rope and used as light rigging. But the operation of simply running in and unloading on the beach became too dangerous. Experience taught that to conceal the tubs on board was not enough; they could be too easily found. Somehow, means had to be devised of getting rid of them completely before the boat came to land, then, if a revenue cutter intercepted just off the shore, the skipper could smile blandly and invite inspection from stem to stern. So the smugglers came in with the tubs fastened by slings to a rope passed round the side of the ship. The rope was weighted and the tubs were provided with a short cord at the upper end with cork markers attached to them. In an emergency it was simple to cast the whole lot adrift and recover the contraband later. As a normal practice some smugglers preferred to get rid of their tubs offshore, leaving them afloat and strung together, for collection by a lighter craft at a suitable time. It was also possible to sink the weighted tubs in shallow water without markers, in which case they would be recovered, by the smugglers or sometimes the revenue men, by means of "peep tubs", empty barrels with a glass bottom for spotting objects underwater, and tongs, creepers or grappling hooks, which were varieties of dragging gear. Smugglers at Bembridge are reported to have tied their tubs together in a raft which was towed in at dead of night by a naked swimmer with a rope round his waist.

Once the goods reached shore, deft organization ensured speedy disposal. A gang would be waiting, a hide-out already chosen, and if a pre-arranged signal told the skipper that it was safe to come right in, the gang would have seized the tubs and, each man with a couple under his arms, would be up the cliffs or stowing them in a cave before a revenue man had time to say "brandy". But there still remained the process of treatment and sale. Here, I feel sure, the stay-at-home wives of Niton played their part, diluting the brandy with fifty per cent water coloured with burnt sugar, bottling some of it for sale to the local unlicensed pop-shops, of which there were four in Niton alone, and arranging transport to the mainland for the rest where it would sell at 50s. a keg, having cost 14s. in Cherbourg.

I have pinned the smuggling trade on Niton, but in fact it seems to have extended from end to end of the Wight. In the mass of literature on this island the smugglers keep cropping up: the smart, patriotic and "upright" sailors at Yarmouth, old washerwomen at Ryde with the bottoms of their baskets lined with bottles, a famous man, Dicky Dawes (with, as we shall see, a yet more famous daughter) operating at St. Helens, early prints of fishermen trundling tubs into the Freshwater caves, the Bembridge folk with their brandy rafts, storage for a hundred tubs in Luccombe Chine, ghost stories (put out by smugglers, of course) among prim ladies at Bonchurch. No wonder that William Arnold, who was Thomas Arnold's father and Collector of Customs at East Cowes, wrote to his Board in October 1783: "We beg leave to report that within the last three months smuggling has increased upon this coast to an alarming degree," and reckoned it a very good month for the Customs if no more than a hundred illicit tubs were landed.

In this "free trade", all the dice were loaded on the side of the smugglers. They could argue that no one outside the government wanted high import duties anyway and their trade was fully in the tradition of British self-help, while their opponents were ignorant tools of authority. Sympathy was everywhere on their side. The revenue men, on the other hand, were thin on the ground, badly paid and wide open to bribery. When they were at sea in their heavy cutters built for all weathers, the smugglers could outsail and, even more easily when the wind was unfavourable, outrow them. Contemporary prints show revenue cutters carrying a vast area of sail to compensate for their broad beam and great depth of keel: a gaff-mainsail hauled out to a long driver boom with two ordinary head-sails, supplemented, when off the wind, with an enormous balloon jib and a square topsail. But still the big cutters were not fast or agile enough, and Acts of Parliament were passed, apparently without much effect, making it an offence for ships to hover less than a certain distance from shore and any boat other than a man-of-war's boat liable to seizure if rowed by more than six oars. And of course, the smugglers always had the initiative. They could choose their own time to make trips and rest between them. Not so their opponents, who had to be on the job all the time, patrolling the shore or the cliffs, by day and night, in all weathers. So weary did they become in their unglamorous duty that they invented a kind of folding seat called the rump- or donkey-stool, and this, it is said, was the father of the modern shooting stick.

Smuggling was rife, of course, along the whole of the English coast, and after the Napoleonic wars, when British command of the sea failed notably to keep the Channel clear of French privateers it was a legitimate precaution for fishing vessels to be armed. In some cases the smugglers took advantage of this to bulldoze their way to shore. This had been happening even in Arnold's time. "Illicit trade", he wrote in the same letter, "is principally carried on in large armed cutters or luggers from two to three hundred tons, with which the revenue cutters are not able to contend. It is no unusual thing for them to land their goods in open day under protection of their guns, sometimes in sight of revenue cutters which they will not suffer to come near or board them." But we are assured that, compared with the mainland, where pitched battles sometimes took place and smuggling craft smothered their opponents with fire, the game was carried on in the island in a fairly sportsmanlike fashion. If that was so, I can only conclude that the revenue men stationed there were not changed often enough and had come to some kind of pact. At any rate, one incautious young man, a new broom perhaps, got into severe trouble. "Whereas", stated an official announcement in 1827, "it has been represented to the Commissioners of His Majesty's Customs that about half-past 10 o'clock on the night of Saturday 30th ultimo, Lt. Arnold of the Atherfield Coast Guard Station fell in with a body of smugglers to the number of 50 or more, coming up the cliffs, many of whom were armed with bludgeons, and that some of the said smugglers attacked him and very much disabled his right hand, a reward of £50 is offered for information . . ." A very high reward, one might think, in those days for anything short of murder, but it shows that it was no good offering chicken-feed to smugglers and a big incentive had to be offered to abandon the trade and become an informer. The profits, in fact, could be immense. Whole rows of houses at Bembridge were built by wealthy smugglers and one man, originally a blacksmith by name Boyce, became so prosperous that he built himself Apley House near Ryde, installed a library though he was practically illiterate and ordered £500 worth of second-hand books from London to line the shelves. For years he escaped the penalty by packing juries with his supporters and it was not until the law was changed, making it necessary to draw jurors' names out of a hat, that he was convicted and sent to prison. At that time he is said to have had £40,000 invested.

I am not sure when smuggling ceased in the Isle of Wight, or whether it has ceased at all. But the great days, when two-thirds of the island population was involved in one way or another, went when duties on brandy, silk and tobacco were lowered and the business became unprofitable. It had never been conquered, it just petered out —leaving innumerable houses along the coast with unwanted cellars, well-trodden cliff paths to be overgrown with gorse, and a crop of stories. Most of them reflect the smugglers' joy at outwitting the revenue men and told to admiring confederates in the pop-shop must have sounded deliriously funny. Today, long after the event, those tales that have reached cold print do not wear so well. But they do show the ingenuity in finding hiding-places. We hear of the revenue men tramping up the path to a certain cottage—panic within, and the smuggler's wife taking to her bed, apparently in her death throes, clasping a tub of brandy to her bosom under the blanket. A farmer on the south coast, when ploughing a field, left a narrow strip untouched in the middle. To a friend he confided: "I've sown her with something different this year, mate"—tubs of brandy. The table-tombs found in many of the island churchyards were very popular as hiding-places. A large family tomb at Mottistone was opened, the coffins were rearranged to provide a space and the tubs hidden beside them. One day before dawn at Niton, some smugglers were coming up from the shore with spirits and bags of tea when the Customs men began to close in on them. They got into the churchyard and when their pursuers had practically encircled it they prised up the slab on one of the tombs and climbed inside with the goods. At daylight, when the enemy had long since given up the chase, a farm labourer was going through the churchyard on his way to work. His son tells the story: "All at once, my father sees the stone slab atop one of the tombs begin to move. He stops short and stares with all his eyes, when up goes the stone higher and a man's face peeps out at one corner and says: 'I say, mate, can you tell me the time?'" In terror, the old man dashed back to the nearest cottage and told the folks: "The Day of Judgement is at hand!" They tried to soothe him, but for hours he sat there quaking, unable to budge, awaiting the sound of the trumpet. . . .

I have spoken to an old man of ninety who was a coastguard at St. Helens during the First World War. There was no smuggling then, but the older people, he said, were still full of these stories. So free trade must have been a fairly recent memory. But by the 1860s, tourists were beginning to flood the island, supplying an alternative source of income. Lucky islanders! They saw their opportunity and seem to have performed the switch very deftly. Along the Under-cliff, where there were innumerable gates along the road, the ex-smugglers were soon standing, cap in hand, ready to open them for the tourists and receive a tip. One old man, though, had a better idea. He simply sat down in his best smock by an open gate with a notice-board above him: "Ninety come Whitsun." He got his pennies as well and perhaps it was to spend them in a worthy fashion that, soon after his birthday, he upped his stool when no one was looking and walked to Newport and back, a distance of sixteen miles, in one day.

But I fear that if we could meet these old-time inhabitants along the Undercliff we would not find them very endearing. They were atrociously inbred, warred frequently with one another, were offensive to strangers and were often drunk. I doubt whether they even noticed the beauties of their surroundings, .though better than anyone since, they knew the cliffs and saw them at all times of the day, in all seasons. But they were not uniquely imperceptive. The Early Victorians, one must remember, went to the seaside for medicinal reasons rather than pleasure and were not great explorers of natural beauty. Young ladies, ever-conscious of decorum, reclined on the beach sometimes and gazed abstractedly at the sea. With more or less enthusiasm they indulged in the uplifting pastimes of archaeology and conchology. They read books from the circulating library and bathed occasionally under a canvas dome lowered from the seaward end of a bathing machine. The young males from whom they were rigorously separated fared little better, except that they bathed by being rowed a discreet distance from the shore and plunging naked into the sea. With animal spirits suppressed, one and all saw the seaside through a film of melancholy and this is painfully obvious from the kind of descriptions which Victorian writers provide. Black tempests, lowering skies, gloomy cliffs were their food. "Awful and sublime" was the Undercliff. They shuddered at the sight of the Needles—"that dreadful promontory whose only inhabitants are gulls and puffins." They were not on friendly terms with nature, they drew from it sustenance for their own subjective feelings and they did not look at it closely.

For us the terrors of the seashore have gone, but it is still difficult for a visitor to appreciate the beauty of the Undercliff because it varies so much with the seasons and it takes time to explore. But there are wonderful colour effects all along this coast. A local artist has described Chale Bay on a late October morning with the sun gilding the cliffs in amber and gold, below, the pearly grey of the blue slipper, and lower still the deep coral red of the fine gravel beach. In June and July, towards sunset, mist often gathers over the coastline, softening the contours of the huge masses of rock and filtering the light so that the sky is daffodil colour and the sea, pale lemon and green. I myself am sorry not to have seen the Undercliff in spring-time when the primroses are out and the trees and shrubs are budding in brilliant green. At such a time one would envy the retired people in their sun-trap houses above the shore, with their intimate view of the Channel, their cute little gardens and a sense of being embedded in awakening nature.

VI

VENTNOR AND THE SOUTH-EAST

VENTNOR is an extraordinary place with an unusual history. It has always had an appeal for me because of its peculiar name, derived, it is suggested, either from the Celtic words *gwent* and *nor* meaning a white beach, or else of Danish origin, and its attraction, mingled with a certain amount of surprise, grew no less when years ago I first saw the place. From the west you can reach it along a top road coming from Newport or else along the leafy tunnel of the Undercliff. The Undercliff approach is the more startling because the drive along that narrow ledge with sheer walls of rock on one side and broken ground falling steeply to the sea on the other convinces you that no town is possible here. Then, suddenly, the tunnel of green comes to an end, the cliffs vanish, the scene opens up, St. Boniface Down rears steeply to its conical peak on your left, and between it and the sea, on a patch only 400 yards wide of rocks, slides, humps, chutes and hollows, Ventnor clings defiantly, like a cluster of man-made barnacles.

The situation is superb, the architecture indomitably Victorian. Down a double S-bend, through the narrow high street, down another formidable gradient with more twists and turns you wriggle your way to the beach, and even to get there seems quite an achievement. Everywhere beside the road are massive stone retaining walls and every conceivable plot in this shuddered and shaken scenery has been levelled and topped with buildings, mostly Victorian ones, stone built, with sash windows and low-pitched, grey slate roofs—Strawberry Hill Gothic, Seaside Swiss and what in Victorian times was known as Carpenter's Palazzo. They face in all directions except north and are slanted at odd angles to catch a glimpse of the sea past walls and chimneys ahead of them. Down by the short esplanade and two-hundred-yard beach are more solid Victorian houses, some fronted by double-tiered wooden balconies and an occasional dusty palm tree. If you climb on foot up the pathways and steps that crawl between the densely packed buildings you come across pocket-handkerchief-sized gardens on walled terraces, chimneys smoke on a level with your head and you pity the postmen who deliver letters on foot in this alpinist's town.

But despite some vistas reminiscent of a penal colony, Ventnor has charm just because it is a museum-piece and an example of total un-planning, if there is such a word. I really don't know, in any case, how planners would go about building a town here for six thousand in-habitants and a flood of summer visitors that found room for them all and was also aesthetically pleasing. The terrace houses are necessary just as sardines must be packed side by side in a tin. And the site, in this sheltered nook of the island, with low, green-topped cliffs reached by meandering paths in echelon to the westward, is so picturesque that you accept the barrack-like buildings as a fairly small debit in the account.

It was the beautiful setting that, a hundred and fifty years ago, first attracted settlers to this corner of the Wight. Making their way on horseback over unmade tracks from Ryde or sailing daringly round the coast, travellers experienced an explorer's thrill as they came on an idyllic scene. Below the towering bulk of St. Boniface lush meadows strewn with rocks tumbled down to sparkling sand where fishermen tended their boats. Above the shore was a tangled, bowl-shaped dell with farm animals and chickens browsing in the undergrowth. Further back, perched high above the beach on a crag stood a thatched, stone-built mill with a water-wheel turned by a stream which fell over rocks in a bubbling cascade to the shore. Beside the mill, lobster pots were piled and fishing nets hung up to dry. One or two rude huts sprinkled the background and further up behind them a large thatched cottage peered between trees. The mill, the waterfall, the huts, the busy scene afforded, wrote one traveller, "a lively and gratifying picture", doubly endearing, no doubt, because of its welcome contrast with the wild, intimidating scenery to the east and west. Here, as distinct from the Undercliff or the formidable Dunnose, where the nights, it was said, were filled with the wails of shipwrecked mariners and the eerie lights of smugglers flickered along the shore, was a scene already half domesti-cated, and to view the enchantment at leisure there was a comfortable inn at hand, the Crab and Lobster. There, after the day's wanderings, the traveller would hear interesting tales from the landlord. Yes, it was the only inn of that name in all England and in 1648 Charles I had visited it when he was not yet a close prisoner in Carisbrooke. Very tired, though, the poor man looked, so the story went, with touches of silver in his hair. Someone at the inn had made a sketch of him in pencil, but the sketch, unfortunately, had been lost.

During and after the Napoleonic wars a succession of eminent people stayed at the cottage among the trees, though not all of them relished the lack of amenities and even fresh crab and lobster began to pall after a while. There was milk and butter to be had on the spot, but the nearest butcher was eight miles away in Brading, a hired postchaise from Ryde, with a boy to open the numerous gates, was expensive at 1s. 6d. a mile, in the whole of this part of the island there was not a single public conveyance, and letters, if they reached Ventnor at all, came by carrier once a week. But in retrospect, it all made the adventure of staying in the wild and secluded spot doubly worth talking about, and talk these gentry undoubtedly did—not least about the truly remarkable climate.

In the 1830s it was the climate, extolled by an eminent physician Sir James Clark, which launched Ventnor on the path to fame. In the gardens of the cottage among the trees and the local inn visitors had already seen myrtles, geraniums, · heliotropes, verbena and petunias surviving the winter out of doors, and they had gone home babbling of the delectable position of the hamlet which was shielded from the southerly gales of autumn and the north-east winds of spring. In Ventnor it was never too hot and never too cold. Frost and snow were meaningless words to the fortunate few, the inhabitants. All this was clothed by Sir James in learned language in his monograph on the climate of the Undercliff. Ailing ladies and gentlemen on that chilly and treacherous island that lay, as Vectensians would have it, as an appendage of the Wight beyond the Solent took due note and before long there was a growing demand for lodgings at what some people were already calling the English Madeira. For the handful of farmers and fishermen who actually lived in the place a rude transformation was at hand.

Half a mile to the west on the Undercliff a mock medieval castle, complete with machiolations, arrow-slits and an embattled gateway with provision for pouring boiling oil on besiegers was being built for a peaceable local landowner, Mr. Hamborough. The builder engaged on this exotic work, today at long last in process of demolition, rented a small plot of land at Ventnor and threw up a cottage for visitors. Other speculators followed his example, buying plots wherever the fancy took them from an absentee and semi-bankrupt owner who, only too glad to see his cash, attached no restrictions to the type of buildings that went up. The race to exploit Ventnor was now on. Sanitary provisions, awkward at any time for the houses that shot up on different levels, were cheerfully disregarded. Where pathways existed these were roughly flattened and then practically squeezed out by the spate of new building. What Victorians themselves called "mean rows of squalid dwellings" soon trailed over the higher levels, while lower down, hotels, shops, cottages and villas began to litter the ground, in every conceivable style, in every outrageous shape.

For some years, until the amenities of the town became established in the 1880s, desperate and sometimes calamitous efforts were made to improve them and cope with the increasing flood of visitors who, beside the growing fame of the Undercliff, were lured by the fact that Queen Victoria had made her home in the island. Only one aspect of health and hygiene was assured, the water supply which came from copious springs in the chalk. But while every sort of conveyance lurched along the Undercliff road at the rate of a thousand a month, yet more thousands of visitors were deterred from coming at all by the difficulty of access, and those that reached the town were not always pleased with the single winding street, the lack of trees or seats for invalids, and the glare from the sea and the whitewashed buildings. Ever-conscious of their gold-mine, the inhabitants sought an Act of Parliament for "paving, lighting, watching, cleansing and otherwise improving the town of Ventnor". That was in the 1840s. But the problem of access proved more difficult and it was not tackled until the 1860s after a further startling rise in the number of summer visitors. It seemed easier to reach Ventnor by sea than by land, so at staggering expense a promontory shielding the little cove from the easterly winds was blasted out of existence and a short timber pier constructed in its place. Here, for a while, steamers from Littlehampton landed passengers and merchandise for the town. It is not, unfortunately, recorded whether pale ladies suffering from corset constricture and clogged lungs found this long sea crossing much of an improvement on the land route from Ryde. However, the alternative soon ceased to exist, the pier collapsed in a gale and the townsmen were confronted with a new and ugly fact. The spit of land so cheerfully removed had acted as a breakwater, preventing thousands of tons of shingle piled against the esplanade from being carried out to sea. Now westerly winds and currents swept the whole lot away, the esplanade, denuded of its bulwark, was battered by eight-foot waves, before long the foreshore was bared right down to the blue slipper and the land along the seafront began to subside. Eventually, the promontory that had been blown sky-high had to be artificially restored and then comparative peace reigned once more along the water-front. But there was still no pier and a permanent one was not built until the 1880s.

Meanwhile, visitors to Ventnor, particularly consumptives drawn by glowing accounts of the climate, could bask, secure from these terrors, several hundred feet above the shore. How, one wonders, did sick people spend their time in a town where two steps from the front door involved precipitous slides and climbs? The fit had plenty to amuse them. There were bathing machines on the shore now, libraries with reading-rooms were spattered about the town, and a gentleman in St. Catherine Street, much recommended as an intelligent companion, was always ready to help sincere enthusiasts search for fossils. The geology of the Wight could be explained after closing time by Mr. Norman, the fishmonger, and Lush, the hairdresser, had a fine collection of moths and butterflies for sale.

Newspaper readers had their alarms, admittedly, and as temporary Wighters they must have felt outraged by an article which appeared in *Vanity Fair* in the '70s. At that time, the Emperor William I of Germany coupled with Bismarck was something of a bugbear. They had smashed France, Denmark and Austria. Germany was an Empire on the make. Where next would they turn their gaze? "We are told", declared *Vanity Fair*, "that Germany proposes to annex the Isle of Wight." But this, according to the paper, would be a blessing. The island was a liability. It required troops from England for its defence. The population was growing so fast that there were people there dying of starvation. "In short, who can look at the history of the Isle of Wight and not see that the lives of the people of England will be much safer and their interests incredibly enhanced by its annexation, with securities for administrative reform, to the great and growing Empire of Germany?" I suppose this was meant as a joke, but I doubt if the islanders, whose memories are long in matters of invasion, found it all that funny, and in the First World War there was, in fact, a widespread belief that the Germans meant to capture the island and use it as a second Heligoland. Then the landladies of Ventnor, sorrowfully eyeing the wild pomegranates, fuchsias, flowering cactus and wild vines with nobody to enjoy them, remembered the flood of German visitors to the town in pre-war days, how the men with their short-cropped hair and thick necks had basked like stranded porpoises on the sand with pebbles on their eyes to protect them from the sun, and wondered how many of them had been there for their health and how many on the business of the Fatherland. Sinister stories there had been about Ventnor natives getting lost on their own downs and being shown the shortest way home by Germans. . . . The fear subsided, but slumbered on, to be revived in the Second World War after the fall of Crete. If Crete could be pocketed in a fortnight, then why not the Isle of Wight?

But the article in *Vanity Fair* was soon forgotten and Ventnor sailed through the '70s and '80s on a rising ride of prosperity. The Royal National Hospital for Diseases of the Chest had been founded in a favoured position in twenty acres of ground and a propaganda broadside delivered by an island doctor before the British Medical Association was really no longer necessary. The climate, he said, was one "in which an open air life may be led even to the extent of having the window of a sleeping apartment partly open at night", and he went on to recommend the island to the "roué, the nervous hypochondriac and the valetudinarian" not only for the climate, but because they could find "constant charm and solace" in visiting the dwelling-places of neolithic men and their tombs on the downs.

The fame of Ventnor, however, was already assured. Karl Marx went there in the last year of his life and was treated for headaches and bronchial trouble by a local doctor, unsuccessfully it seems, for on returning to London Marx wrote to him in a cramped and curiously juvenile hand, complaining of his symptoms and adding ruefully: "Mere moral agencies do not, I suppose, touch the movements of the mucus." In the spring of 1878, a small boy named Winston Churchill came with his mother. From the cliffs he saw a splendid ship sail past within a mile or two of the shore. She was H.M.S. *Eurydice*, of 920 tons and four guns, homeward bound from Bermuda and crammed with troops looking forward to their leave. At that moment, a storm sprang up with violent wind and snow and the young Winston was hustled to shelter. Next time he went to the cliffs there was no splendid ship with spread of sail but three black masts rearing out of the water. Struck with her gun-ports open by the sudden squall, the *Eurydice* had reeled, taking in tons of water, righted herself and then, being struck again, had suddenly foundered with the loss of over three hundred lives. Only two seamen had been saved. This was the worst disaster in the history of island wrecks, and in *My Early Life* Sir Winston records that the story of divers finding corpses being eaten by fishes left a scar on his mind.

But meanwhile, neighbouring Bonchurch was also becoming famous as a resort, Bonchurch that nestles even more closely than Ventnor under a rugged spur of St. Boniface Down, on an even narrower shelf that slopes yet more steeply to the sea, a small, supremely picturesque village with great lumps of rock that long ago came crashing from the cliff behind, with gurgling streams, cascading lawns and undergrowth of almost tropical luxuriance. Ventnor looks naked, but Bonchurch is thickly clothed with trees that stand sentinel in the delicious grounds of opulent villas, straggle down to the shore and soften the prospect of the menacing rock at the foot of the down.

All the same, I would not like to live in Bonchurch because there is too much grey stone, and except in bright weather when the sun and the glistening sea provide escape the village has a slightly claustrophobic air. But there is certainly fascination here of every kind, and not the least derives from a genuine paradox. Even now, with access up bottom-gear roads to the east and west, Bonchurch seems cut off from the world, saved from stagnation only by the sea and a stirring in the tops of the trees. If you drop down into the village on a December day, warm, soft air laps your face and it is like tunnelling into cotton wool. You feel you are in a little Shangri-La where people will speak more slowly, live more quietly, where sleep will be dreamless, the sea-sounds playing all night in the ear, and where sometime, silently and without fuss, you will embark for eternity which is only a few steps away in the yard, rampant with wild flowers, of the age-old church. Even today, with cars, telephones and the rest, you feel this isolation. But in former ages it was real, to the modern mind terribly real and complete. Yet, and here is the paradox, the eye of history has shone more than once on Bonchurch and for at least the last two centuries it has had various links with the outside world. When the pagan Saxons fished in the bay a young and earnest man from Hampshire with divine fire in his eyes came and preached to them of Christ. Winfrid was his name and, years later, after he had been martyred in East Friesland and made a saint, he gave his name to the down and the village. After the Conquest, monks from Lyra in Normandy, to which abbey William FitzOsbern had attached six island churches, landed on the shore below Bonchurch to collect their tithes, giving it its present name of Monks' Bay. Then there was the French invasion of 1545 and in the eighteenth century, as elsewhere in the island, smuggling was rife in the village. The brandy-casks were easy to carry, one under each arm, being only about fourteen inches long with a circumference at the top the size of a tea plate and in a cave under the cliffs known as Old Jack there was room for upwards of five hundred at a time. St. Boniface would hardly have been edified by the lawless behaviour in his parish, neither would he have condoned the practices that sprang up in later years: the lads of Ventnor and Bonchurch climbing his down on Sundays to hold a free fight on the top, pilgrimages to St. Bonny's well, a clear spring gushing high up out of the chalk, which once a year was garlanded with flowers by the local maidens, and the strong whiff of paganism which continues even today in the prose and poetry of Bonchurch authors who in recent times have been the village's strongest link with a wider world. De Vere Stacpoole half believed that wild strawberries were plucked from his garden for fairy banquets, ghosts and little green men that sometimes were found stripping the gooseberry bushes came easily to his pen, and Alfred Noyes wrote of phantom ships sailing past, their holds loaded with phantom gold. As for Swinburne, the last of the great Victorian poets, who was born here and was buried in the new churchyard, who can doubt that it was from this dozing plot that he drew his inspiration for a sleep of eternal peace when "even the weariest river winds somewhere safe to sea".

Today Bonchurch is indomitably residential, as distinct from Ventnor where the trippers and holiday-makers go, but it was a long time before the village acquired nocturnal respectability and it is a great pity that Gilbert could not have seen it in the 1830s and '40s when the change was taking place. What a theme for a comic opera! By day, "romantic old maids fond of novels, or soldiers' widows with a pretty jointure, or anybody's widows or aunts given to poetry and a pianoforte", as Keats described a recent influx of gentility, could take the air, sniff the honeysuckle or gather roses, untroubled by the harsh facts of life—and these were that practically every one of the fisher-folk who so amiably touched their caps by day was converted into a smuggler at night. As soon as the silk went indoors, the blue serge got to work and the darkness was full of footsteps, bumps and curses. Behind shuttered windows the widows and aunts listened with a fearful surmise: could it be that the place was haunted? Soon, sure enough, there were stories of a phantom coach that trundled along the lower road, stopped at one of the cottages by the pond and then passed on, to vanish along the Undercliff. Then there was a horse that someone had seen padding noiselessly like a fox with fire belching from its nostrils. One night, a servant sent late from one of the big houses to fetch a doctor from Newport actually met the horse, struck at it with his whip, whereupon the animal divided into half and then neatly vanished. Did the smugglers help these stories along? Why, of course: with pads for the horses' hooves and a touch of phosphorus for the nostrils, above all with whispered tales dropped here and there: "They do say that about this time of year . . ."

With its scenic beauty it is not surprising that this part of the Wight has drawn imaginative writers like a honey-pot. Noyes and Stacpoole both lived in Bonchurch. Tennyson stayed long enough to have his sombrero sliced into mementoes by a bevy of female admirers. Dickens began *Great Expectations* there, while round the corner at Shanklin Keats stayed at a cliff-top house where there is now a promenade called Keats Green and wrote "Lamia", "Otho the Great" and, incidentally, a description in pedestrian prose of the famous chine —which was perhaps all it deserved. In 1868, when Shanklin still had only a few hundred inhabitants, Longfellow drifted in and out, admired the old village and the charms of the chambermaid at Holliers Hotel, and wrote some sentimental verses to a drinking fountain. Mindful of these famous literati, a less well known writer described the village at that time as "sweet with shadow, leafy twitterings, the murmur of a prattling streamlet and"—running out of colourful adjectives—"the fall of a tiny waterfall."

This seems odd to us now, but Sandown-Shanklin did not really start moving until the 1870s. Twenty years previously, Shanklin had only 355 inhabitants, which was precisely 255 more than the population in 1790. The old village, which still exists as a charming cluster of thatched cottages, was the whole of Shanklin and at that same period, at the mid-century, Sandown had even fewer houses. "A village by a sandy shore", declared a writer whose muse on other parts of the island never forsook him—and then dried up completely. I wish he had described the village in detail, gone into the cottages, talked to the people and written down what they said, for that would have given us an insight into life in at least one corner of the Wight, and so by extension to the whole island. If the past is to come to life, someone, somewhere, must have concentrated his gaze and recorded everything he saw and heard. But no one ever did. So bygone Sandown and Shanklin slip by; not a face, not a whisper survive. Instead, we hear without undue excitement that, towards the end of his life, John Wilkes, the rake and Member of Parliament who in the 1760s unintentionally became the champion of English freedom from arbitrary arrest, led an eccentric existence at Sandown, dazzled the farmers' daughters in a suit of scarlet trimmed with gold, sired numerous illegitimate offspring and cooled his wine in a memorial in imitation of Virgil's tomb which he erected to a poet friend. But for me, despite colourful attributes, Wilkes refuses to come to life and if I stayed in this area today I should be unlikely to go in search of his "villakin", if it is still there. I would much rather sit on Shanklin beach and picture two of Dickens' characters as they come trailing past—Mr. and Mrs. Lammle from *Our Mutual Friend*. They are not arm-in-arm as they ought to be, considering that they are on their honeymoon, but in fierce altercation, she jabbing her parasol in the wet sand, he twitching his ginger moustaches. Each had been led to believe that the other was a person of property and each has married the other for that reason. Alas, the truth is that neither has a bean. This is the situation, they have just discovered it, and both are understandably indignant. "Do you pretend to believe", we hear her declare, "when you talk of my marrying you for worldly advantages that it was within the bounds of reasonable probability that I would have married you for yourself?!" No, Mr. Lammle does not think that, but neither was it her blue eyes alone which attracted him to her. They both ought to face the facts, he suggests. Why, since both need money and have failed to get it from this match, should they not sink their differences and combine in a business-like way to obtain it? At first she is not impressed. But then, with a bad grace but a dawning hope, she agrees. Then both step out more briskly and at last, between the cliffs and the laughing sea—laughing in mockery?—they vanish from sight. . . .

In August 1880, the famous French poet and novelist, Paul Bourget, stayed in Shanklin. He found it picturesque, prosperous and respectable, a "classical village of English romance" with velvet-smooth lawns and pretty cottages covered with rambler roses. In the bright, comfortable rooms he pictured respectable folk endlessly drinking tea, but not talking because he could not imagine these English people saying much, even in their own homes. On the esplanade, melancholy, dark-clothed persons paced up and down, occasionally uttering a phrase between half-clenched teeth. On Keats Green, where a soft summer moon vied with the gas jets, a band played in the evenings, the musicians wearing a metal epaulette to which was hooked a small lantern. This performance was eyed solemnly by a crowd of mothers and young people. But week-day solemnity was at least enlivened by the occasional cricket match where everybody turned up dressed to the nines, even the non-playing men in white flannels. The only trouble was, the Frenchman was still expecting the game to begin when apparently it had ended. But on Sundays everything clamped down. The shops were all shut, by early morning all the bathing machines had been drawn up under the cliff, pleasure boats vanished from the sea and restaurants refused to serve intoxicants. Gravely the populace proceeded to church. There were already four churches in Shanklin then, and four more were building. The service lasted for an hour and a half. The parson read his sermon in a monotone, the congregation droned the hymns. Not a whisper, not a smile. And when a young lady offered to share her hymn-book with him, Bourget was astounded to note no air of coquetry, no ulterior motive, nothing, apparently, but the desire to perform a pious deed. "If belief," he wrote, "is not sincere in every heart, it is at least sincere in outward appearance."

When I visit Shanklin today I am astounded to think of that universal Victorian gravity. Could people really have been so consistently solemn beside the glittering sea, those dancing waves? And what about the children? Did they not gambol and fool about with bucket and spade? There were laughs, of course, and there were gambols, but Victorian children's books show that the fun was always carefully controlled, interlarded with object lessons and instructive dicta about fossils and varieties of seaweed. If there was a hilarious party it took place in private with a sense of guilt hanging heavy in the atmosphere at being so abandoned. Self-abandon in public was dangerous for class divisions and dangerous to the entrenched position of the Victorian male. Solemnity was safe and it was respectable, and to be respectable was half-way to being refined. That was the equation. At Ryde, Bourget noted much refinement, against an upper-class background of huge fuchsias and hothouse plants growing in the open, multi-coloured flower-beds, smooth lawns and opulent houses. To his amazement, throughout his stay in the island he saw not one man in working clothes, not one barefoot child begging alms, and this, he thought, was because the English, "those unsurpassable artists in comfort", had carefully banished such reminders of work and poverty from their garden-isle.

But here, I am sure, Bourget was miles off the target. At that time there were no industrial workers in the island and no one had need to beg. The squalor of England's factory towns was unknown here. In the 1860s, agricultural labourers had been earning from 7s. to 12s. a week, while the rent of their cottages, practically all of which had decent-sized gardens, was only two guineas a year. Since the turn of the century, population had been steadily rising. In 1801, it had been 22,000; by 1881 it was nearly 74,000. Not all this could be accounted for by natural increase. There were many immigrants and as few people came to the island to fish or work on the land, except seasonally in the harvest month, they must have belonged to the leisured classes. These people helped to swell the population of the seaside towns and give them their air of prosperous respectability. The biggest influx came when the island railways were starting up and in the ten years from 1861 the population grew by nearly a thousand a year, a rate of increase never equalled before or since. This was the period when the rash of Victorian building spread which some writers have declared spoiled the island for ever.

Before the wave of immigration and the advent of the railways brought uniformity and ironed out local characteristics, the little island communities were as self-sufficient as cells in a honeycomb. Within these cells each family led a cloistered, home-made life. Roland Prothero, later Lord Ernle, whose father was rector of Whippingham, spent his childhood on the far side of this great divide in the 1850's and describes the life in his autobiography. When people came to stay at the rectory, which was not particularly inaccessible, the visit was arranged weeks beforehand through the post. There were no mechanical means of transport on the island in those days, not so much as a bone-shaker bicycle, and for casual calls eight miles was considered a prohibitive distance. So the family was much cast on its own resources. Groceries were unobtainable locally and had to be sent from London. Bread was baked, soap was made and beer was brewed on the premises. Strangers were hardly ever seen and the only people who relieved the monotony of local faces were the professional wayfarers: the pedlar with his pack full of trays like a diminutive chest of drawers, and the organ-grinder whose instrument had a row of dancing marionettes in a glass case on the top. These people were a substitute for entertainments taken for granted now, but then very limited. Bridge had not yet been invented, lawn tennis did not arrive till ten years later, croquet was only just coming in and golf was unheard of in the south of England. So to amuse themselves and incidentally their parents the children dressed up and performed traditional mummers' plays—by the light of wax candles downstairs and tallow candles in the nursery.

But at any rate, in Prothero's childhood the steam packet to the mainland was in operation and Portsmouth was linked to London by rail. Transport for goods and people was faster, more reliable and cheaper, and it was the high cost which had previously forced almost complete self-sufficiency on the islanders. In Bembridge, for instance, flax, canvas for sails and iron were the only materials that had to be imported from over the water. All the bread was made of home-grown wheat, stone-ground. Mutton and pork had always been plentiful in the island. Beer was brewed in the village and it need hardly be said that good French brandy, Hollands gin and tobacco could always be obtained from the smugglers. For boat-building nothing was better than island wych elm or Bembridge oak, and so conscious were local people of the fact that they used to go around with acorns in their pockets and stick them in the ground in likely places so that their descendants would have a good supply of timber. Copper nails were made at Ryde and ropes at Seaview. House-building presented no problems; stones from the beach or locally·made bricks were used for the walls, the lime for the mortar was burnt under the downs and island timber provided the woodwork. Boots were made of leather supplied by the village tanner and all outer clothing was of homespun, the flax being made up into linen so durable that one smock and three shirts were reckoned to equip a man for a lifetime. Salt, too, was prepared in the island, not only for home consumption, but for export to London, and with salt duties as high sometimes as thirty or forty times the value of the product this, until the opening of the Cheshire salt mines, was a very lucrative trade. Until the early 1900s a heavy, four-horse waggon could still be seen near Bembridge known as the salt wain which at one time had made periodic trips to London from Barnsley saltern, a couple of miles away. There the salt was extracted by letting sea-water into a number of pools connected by sluices. As the water passed from one to the other, it got more salty by evaporation until the final stage was reached when the brine was dried out in shallow pans over a fire. That the resultant mess could be called salt by verbal association is clear; equally clearly it could not be called sodium chloride—and the taste must have been horrible.

It may be that the self-sufficiency of Bembridge was outstanding among island villages because of its position. A glance at the map will show that it is very much out on a limb at the easternmost point of the Wight and in Norman times this limb was completely separated from the main body of the island by the sea which extended all over the flat land from between Sandown and Culver Cliff to Brading harbour. Instead of the modern harbour there was a navigable channel which lapped the walls of Brading itself and the village was an important trading centre known as "the Kyng's Towne of Bradynge" with a sizeable population. Bembridge in those early days was very small. But periodically and at long intervals attempts were made to reclaim the land. In 1336 an embanked causeway was built at Yarbridge, south of Brading, as a first step towards shutting out the sea from the south. Centuries later the local gentry started work on the north side until in the reign of James I a major attempt at reclamation was made by Sir Andrew Middleton who had constructed the New River to supply the City of London with water. High profits were expected from the enterprise, £7,000 was spent, thousands of tons of earth were unloaded. Hopefully, Sir Andrew planted rape seed on the poor sandy soil reclaimed, built a watermill, a barn and a house—and then wisely sold his share in the scheme. Soon after, the sea broke through the embankment and the land was flooded again. But partial success had been achieved and in later years, inspired perhaps by the discovery of a well cased with stone in the middle of the area which showed that it had once been dry land, the local people repaired the embankment, carted further tons of earth and gradually began to win the battle with the sea. By the late eighteenth century, maps show that the sea channel had now been reduced to a long, bulbous arm extending inland from Brading harbour to within a mile of the village. In that state, still flooded at high tide, the area was useless for agriculture, but only one more big effort was needed and the sea was shut out altogether. In 1878 the present outline of Brading harbour was established when, amid resounding financial scandals, a sea-wall was built on the inland side. Behind this, a few years later, a branch railway line was built from Brading to Bembridge, so linking the still modest little community with Ryde and Ventnor.

That was the beginning of Bembridge as a holiday resort, and today it has an official guide all to itself, boasting of its sunshine, its yachting facilities and its 3,000 inhabitants. In this guide Brading harbour is called Bembridge harbour, which I suppose is more accurate today. Brading is given one short paragraph and St. Helens, on the opposite side of the harbour, is praised for its cattle and geese "which graze on the rough grass by ancient right"—and for its cricket and football clubs, which presumably graze on smooth grass by modern concession.

But this really will not do for St. Helens, which was an important and prosperous place when the Bembridgeans were pottering about on their peninsula, casting envious glances across the ooze of Brading harbour. In 1795, there were 40 houses and about 200 people in St. Helens, but fifty years later the population had risen to nearly 2,000, and this was because of the Royal Navy. In the Napoleonic wars the fleet used to rendezvous off the village rather than in Spithead, and warships anchored there for longish periods, for two good reasons. Ships could hardly sail to windward at all in those days so that if they were to move down-Channel a two or three weeks' wait for a fair wind was sometimes necessary. For this purpose St. Helens Roads, sheltered from the west, were a much more comfortable place to wait in than Spithead. But also, every newly commissioned warship needed a period of working up, and because the crew would contain pressed men or drafted prisoners it would be necessary to put to sea as soon as possible to prevent them escaping. So the working up was not done in harbour, but the ships came round to St. Helens where they anchored a safe distance off-shore and the crews were then trained in managing the sails and firing the guns. This brought great prosperity to the village. St. Helens water was much in demand as it possessed some property that prevented it going brackish after long periods at sea, and when the fleet was in there was often a demand for immediate delivery of fifty locally killed bullocks, as well as mutton, beer, poultry and eggs for the officers' tables. The only drawback was the press-gang which was very active here owing to the proximity of the warships, and it is said that the men of the village lived in constant dread of being hauled off for a seafaring life aboard a man-of-war where the chances of concealing brandy tubs in the bilges would be slender indeed. The seriousness of this danger is shown by the fact that they even installed a cannon on the shore which was fired in warning when the press-gang landed so that the men could have time to hide in the woods.

There is a story, too, about the origin of the word "holystone". A sailors' adage used to run:

"Six days shalt thou labour and do all that thou art able,
And on the seventh holystone the decks and scrape the cable."

The sand for rubbing the decks came from St. Helens shore and odd pieces of stone from the old and derelict church were used for applying it—hence, it is said, the word "holystone".

But the fame of St. Helens does not rest only on these matters and a modern villager would be unlikely to wax enthusiastic on the subject of the vanished prosperity, the press-gang or the holystone. More probably he would say to you: "Have you ever heard of Sophie Dawes?" And you would say to him: "Never." Then he would give an ambiguous smile and take you to a cottage where there is a tablet over the door which reads: "Sophie Dawes, Madame de Fouchères, Daughter of Richard Dawes, Fisherman and Smuggler, known as the Queen of Chantilly, was born here about 1792." And then perhaps he would say: "I could lend you a book about her, if you like. It's a very interesting story."

VII

A GIRL FROM ST. HELENS

Now this chapter, I must warn you, is a slight digression. But the story of Sophie Dawes is so fantastic that I cannot resist telling it. The book was by Marjorie Bowen and published in 1935. It was the product of patient research, was carefully documented and proved, I should imagine, a considerable shock to the people of St. Helens. Up till then they had basked in the reflected glory of what they thought to be the unsullied tale of the local girl that had made good: sweet little Sophie, the smuggler's daughter, who had risen above her circumstances, picked up a wealthy foreign gentleman, gone to Paris with him, nursed his old age and, after his death, returned, rich of course, but with her big kind heart still thumping away, to shower benefits on her kith and kin, give the rest of her fortune to charity and then die herself, dropsical but very pious, in London. Such was the tale, such the local legend. But Sophie, as it happened, was not that sort of a girl.

Dicky Dawes was her father, oyster-catcher of St. Helens who was famous locally for his smuggling feats in brandy, silk and tobacco. Near a spot called the Cole are some rocks still marked on charts as Dicky Dawes Banks and the passage between them is called Dicky Dawes Gut. In 1775 he married a St. Helens girl named Jane Calloway and at long intervals children arrived, first a son and then two daughters, Sophie being born last in 1792. But as a smuggler Dicky had, of course, to sample his wares and soon after the turn of the century he died, full of fame and brandy, leaving a destitute family. Winkle-gathering on Bembridge beach was not enough to keep them alive and they were taken to the House of Industry at Parkhurst, a progressive kind of workhouse where the inmates were well cared for and given employment on the premises. When Sophie was thirteen she went to work for a local farmer. A couple of years later, she walked out on him and went to Portsmouth, where she worked as a chambermaid at the George Hotel. The next rung in the ladder was London, assistant in a milliner's shop, which she was shortly forced to leave after an affair with a young water-carrier. Then came Covent Garden, selling oranges and even, it is said, appearing on the stage. But whichever the role, plump Sophie was quite a tall girl by now, with rich brown hair, pure complexion, regular features and large, dark blue eyes, and she did not go unnoticed; she is next chronicled in the arms of an anonymous gentleman, installed in an elegant villa at Turnham Green. He tired of her quickly, it seems, but at this first crisis in her career young Sophie showed her mettle and we next hear of her performing non-professional functions at a brothel in Piccadilly, settled by another anonymous gentleman with £50 a year. There a certain Monsieur Guy, servant to the exiled Duc de Bourbon, spotted her and spoke of her to his master. This was the turning-point in her fortunes.

The Duke was then fifty-two and, since the murder of his son, the Duc d'Enghien, at Napoleon's orders, the last of the Condés. One can excuse him for feeling somewhat dejected in London at that time, not knowing whether he would ever see his fabulous wealth across the water again or would ever inherit from his even wealthier father, the Prince de Condé. Moreover he was lonely and by nature weak and easily influenced. The bright, bouncing Sophie, when he met her, seemed just the person to inject him with new vigour and hope for the future. Graciously he gave her his patronage, eagerly she seized it, and apart from a brief aberration when he is said to have played cards with the Duke of Kent (later, Queen Victoria's father) with the fair Sophie as stake he seems to have done his very best for her. The year 1812 finds her in a splendid house off Queen's Square, Bloomsbury, with £800 a year settled as pin-money, being educated·at her lover's expense: French, Latin, Greek, music, singing, dancing and deportment. Deportment, as later events were to prove, was always her weak subject, but she must have mastered enough French to discover for herself, if she did not already know, just *who* her kind gentleman was and how glittering were her prospects. There and then, we can safely presume, she resolved to stick to him, through thick, through thin.

But then came 1814 and the restoration in France. The Duke could not get back to Paris fast enough. Tearing himself away from the tearful Sophie, he set sail, leaving her literally and metaphorically on the beach. A fateful moment. But Sophie wasted no time in regrets and the same year found her in Paris, showering the Duke with letters liberally spattered with the expression, "you poor dear", which shows that she was pursuing the line, psychologically right on target, that she alone understood him and could protect him in a difficult and dangerous world. But though these tactics were ultimately successful, they were slow to produce results—at least, the results that Sophie wanted—and in the next four years there seem to have been occasional meetings, but at her lodgings and not at the Duke's home where she was longing to get a foothold. Then in 1818 his father died and vast wealth, together with the title of Prince, descended on the poor dear: the Palais Bourbon in Paris and estates at Chantilly, Enghien, Guise and Montmorency. The same year found her at last in the Palais Bourbon in earnest consultation with her lover. "Together again!" we can hear her say in her charming St. Helens French. "Never must we be separated! It would be too cruel, too tragic, and so terribly bad for you, you poor dear!" What she wanted was open acknowledgement that she was now *maîtresse en titre*. But to this the Prince demurred. Private acknowledgement, yes; she could live in the house, but not as his official mistress. These were awkward stipulations. But triumphantly Sophie found a way out. She would come and live at the palace as Madame Sophie Clarck, widow of William Dawes, one-time agent of the British India Company and daughter of——? Oh, anybody: daughter of Richard Clarck, Esquire (a knight's son, therefore) of Southampton. But to the Prince this did not seem quite proper, either, and he cast round for some alternative scheme. Who suggested the final solution is not known, but it was decided that the Prince should pronounce Sophie to be his illegitimate daughter and that she should also get married, for the sake of good form, to some suitably impeccable, but not too possessive young gentleman. Thus she could come and live openly at the palace and not a breath of scandal would touch the happy ménage.

So in that year the girl from St. Helens was married in London (why London is not clear) to a Monsieur de Fouchères, an officer in Louis XVIII's Guards and described as full of distinction and honour. Then the happy couple hastened back to Paris where the doors of the Palais Bourbon were open for them both, ·there was a job in the household for the husband and many privileges for the Prince's "illegitimate daughter". She was able to go everywhere in society with him, except to Court which the King kept firmly barred to her. She was surrounded with luxury and the infatuated Prince watched fondly while she simpered her way through private theatricals in which she always played the leading parts herself. Good enough, one might think, for a simple winkle-picker from the Isle of Wight and Sophie could afford to relax. And with her goal achieved, relax indeed she did—to reveal the substratum of her charm, hitherto carefully concealed: inordinate vanity and a suspicious, quarrelsome, noisy, vulgar, grasping and domineering nature.

Soon the Prince, now aged sixty to her twenty-six and never a forceful man, became seriously alarmed. She tweaked him by the ear, she shouted at him, she dominated him entirely and there was more than a streak of sheer brutality in her temperament which made him physically afraid. It was this combination of his weakness and her strength which produced a truly extraordinary situation at the Palais Bourbon. There was a very large household, but in time Sophie, like some ruthless Amazon, brought all the key figures under her control. The Prince's hairdresser became her lover, a disreputable Abbé who tended to his spiritual needs, her devoted admirer. From London her nephew James Dawes, a beefy young meat porter, was fetched over at her insistence, installed in the household, styled the Baron de Flassans and made the Prince's first equerry. Soon, her mother, Jane née Calloway, was brought from St. Helens, given comfortable lodgings in Paris and the fatuous Prince was calling her "Grandmama". Next, Mary Anne, Sophie's elder sister, arrived, a suitable husband was found for her, a Captain-Adjutant-Major, whatever that may be, the Prince gave her a dowry of 100,000 francs and the couple also set up house in Paris. All this, no doubt, from Sophie's powerful urge to monopolize the Prince, his wealth and his far-flung possessions throughout France. The whole glittering mass represented a winkle of gigantic proportions; she had her pin and was determined it should all be hers.

Then something awkward occurred. At last her husband, the trusting M. Fouchères, got wind of her relationship with the Prince. There was a thunderous scene; at first Sophie denied everything, but finally shouted in his face: "All right, I am not the Prince's daughter, but his mistress—so there!" In a towering rage the husband fetched a horsewhip and there was an ugly interview from which Sophie emerged bruised, hysterical, but utterly unrepentant. Having fulfilled his duty as an officer full of distinction and honour, M. Fouchères then left the palace. There was a divorce, Sophie became the talk of the town and she was hissed in her scarlet turban at the opera. The Prince was, of course, much displeased and it may well be that Sophie now began to detect a certain resistance to her bullying as though the worm were about to turn.

It was at this moment that she did some serious thinking. She had luxury—granted. Her mother, her sister and her nephew, most of the Dawes family in fact, were also well in the clover. But what of the future? At sixty-five or thereabouts, the old worm was not wearing well and he had not yet, as she knew, made a will. If he did, in his present state of mind, her prospects might be none too good. One day, she might find herself on the street again, penniless except for some jewellery, with only her fading charms. Something must be done.

Sophie concocted a cunning scheme. The first thing was to get the Prince to make a will, if possible leaving her a substantial fortune, but at any rate leaving her something. To swell this something into sizeable proportions she devised another string to her bow. She knew that the Duke of Orleans (later King Louis Philippe) was not well-to-do, and she guessed that his youngest son, the Duke of Aumale, would be badly provided for. Would it be possible, she wondered, to persuade her Prince to make Aumale his universal heir? If that could be done, and known to be done through her, she could obtain a substantial cut from the Orleans family. Then, whatever happened, she would keep well afloat.

As soon as she had thought up this scheme, Sophie started to put it into effect. The first step was to contact Louis Philippe, win his confidence, propound the plan and get his blessing on it. The entrée to the Orleans household was obtained through Talleyrand who, intrigued perhaps by the gutter-queen, consented to act as intermediary and even put up with her at long tête-à-tête dinners. An introduction to the Palais Royal followed. Louis Philippe was enchanted—by Sophie avowedly and by the plan undoubtedly. Soon the young Duke of Aumale was being presented to her while the bystanders cooed: "Deign, Madame, to embrace your protégé!"

But there was not much love lost between the Bourbons and the Orleans and with the stubbornness of advancing senility the "poor dear" proved difficult to handle. He would not make a will, let alone declare the young Aumale his heir. Furious, Sophie applied moral and even physical pressure. She slammed doors in his face and sometimes screams and shouts could be heard coming from their apartments, the

Luccombe Common

old man quavering at her: *"Canaille! Intrigante!"* The wearisome struggle went on for years. The Prince hated her, but dared not send her packing. "I am a fly", he would say, "caught in her web." At last, in August 1829, a wreck of a man now, suffering from insomnia following a partial stroke, with gout and a weak heart, he signed a will, making the Duke of Aumale his universal heir, which meant leaving him a fortune of between 75 and 80 million francs. Sophie was told that she was to receive 12 million.

No sooner had he confided this than the Prince began to fear for his life, and with good reason. His doctors had ordered him a light diet. Sophie promptly changed this prescription into heavy food with much Chambertin and champagne. But the old man—at least this revenge was open to him—ate and drank all, and survived. Soon after, Sophie realized one of her major ambitions. In the last year of his reign, Charles X agreed to receive her at court. The triumph, though, was an empty one. The courtiers snubbed her and the King, though polite, merely remarked to her on the coldness of the weather. But even that, if she had any humility left in her, might have seemed enough to Sophie: from St. Helens to: *"Il fait froid, n'est-ce pas?"* from royal lips. . . .

But Charles himself was a Bourbon and when the July revolution of 1830 forced him into exile, the aged Prince began bitterly to regret having made the new king's son his heir. Obviously, Aumale would now lack for nothing; Charles X's grandson, on the other hand, the Duke of Bordeaux, might well be left penniless. At St. Leu, one of his country estates, the horrified Sophie saw the old man fumbling with legal documents, writing a lot and consulting his lawyers. It did not take her long to find out that he was planning to make another will leaving everything to the Duke of Bordeaux, and then to flee secretly to the coast, cross to England and join Charles X in exile. Stark ruin faced her! So long as the Prince stayed at St. Leu, where her spies were all about him, she was confident of being able to stop the new will. But if he left without her, he might spatter the country-side with wills, not one of them leaving her a bean, or putting the Orleans in her debt. Secretly, therefore, when she heard of his plan she had another carriage held in readiness so that she could pursue him if he fled. Then she informed Louis Philippe of this sinister trend in events and back came the answer: "Stop him at all costs."

Meanwhile, she said nothing to the Prince and let him go ahead

Carisbrooke Castle
The well-house

with his plans. All was ready for him to leave on 27th August, 1830. Their last evening together was very cosy. Both were in good humour, the Prince because he believed he would soon be rid of Sophie, and Sophie because she had no intention of letting him. So they amiably played cards, both in happier mood than the game itself warranted, Sophie perhaps cheating him of a last few francs. . . .

Next morning, when a servant came to wake the Prince, a grotesque scene met his eyes. The dead body of the old man was suspended rather than hanging by two handkerchiefs tied round the neck and attached to a crossbar of the French windows. Obviously, and at the first glance, this was a feeble attempt to make out that the Prince had hanged himself. But his toes were still touching the carpet and the noose round his neck was wide enough for the servant to slip his hand through it. There was no sign of bruising on the skin and even if the noose had been tight enough to produce strangulation, the old man had been much too weak even to dress and undress himself, let alone string himself up like a chicken. Never was there a clearer case of murder, a more obvious suspect or a clearer motive.

As soon as the servant announced his discovery, the bedroom was flooded with people, lamenting or cynically curious, depending on whether they were loyal to the Prince or to Sophie. Quickly she emerged from her own bedroom, professed horror and shock, squeezed out a few tears and as quickly recovered her poise. Meanwhile, the body was slipped from the noose and amid the general confusion all clues that might have led to the murderer were destroyed, intentionally or otherwise. There was one fact, though, that could not be overlooked. There were two ways of entering the Prince's bedroom. One was by the main door which was always guarded at night by a lackey who slept outside. The other was by a secret door which was usually kept bolted on the inside. Now, on the morning after the crime, it was found unbolted.

For a few hours, while argument raged as to the cause of the Prince's death, Sophie kept up a mask of puzzled concern, only letting it slip once when the will was opened and she voiced her disgust at the dead "wretch" who had indeed made the King's son his heir, but had left her only two million francs instead of twelve. Then, without waiting for the police and their awkward questions, she set off for Paris with her current lover, a portly sergeant in the Gens d'Armes, concealed in her carriage. She knew what she had to do: consult Louis Philippe at once. It was he who had said: "Stop him at all costs", and the Prince had been effectively stopped. It was up to the King now to give her protection. At the Palais Bourbon in Paris it seemed for a while as though she was losing her nerve. She made armed men sleep outside her bedroom and was on the verge of hysterics. But she quickly recovered and, ignoring the jeers which followed her wherever she went, was frequently seen, overdressed, blousy and severe, driving with myriads of servants to the royal palace where Louis Philippe and his Queen received her warmly. Their conversation cannot have been confined to platitudes, either, because when an inquiry into the death was finally held, the Prince was declared, in the teeth of all the evidence, to have committed suicide. But this did not put a stop to rumours and soon it was being openly said in Paris that Sophie was a murderess and thief and her accomplice was the King himself. This story was powerfully supported by the fact that all the magistrates and leading officials who had helped to procure the verdict were suddenly given preferment.

There the matter might have rested, a sordid tragedy in which a simple winkle-picker from the Isle of Wight had severely compromised the King of France. But though the dead Prince had no direct heir, there was a nearest male relative, his cousin-german, Prince Louis de Rohan, and when he heard that he had been left nothing in the will he challenged it in the courts as having been made under undue influence—whose influence was never in doubt. The case opened in Poitouse, but was then transferred to the highest court in Paris. Sophie had to give evidence—there was nothing the King could do to prevent this—and her enemies from the old Prince's household painted a devastating picture of her rule: the violence, the vulgarity, the angry scenes, her ruthless domination, the house stuffed with her toadies, the old man isolated in his own home—in short, a reign of naked terror. Gradually, against this background, the whole interest of the case returned to the question of the Prince's death, which was in any case relevant to the issue. Enough had already been said to make the verdict of suicide seem very doubtful and the presiding judge, as it happened, was a conscientious man, not to be intimidated.

The judge probed and cross-questioned, more witnesses were called, and one of them, a game-keeper, told a story highly compromising for Sophie. Years before, by a leafy glade at Chantilly, he had seen two people walking past, Sophie and her nephew the "Baron de

Flassans". They were discussing the old Prince's will, and he had heard the lady say: "It wouldn't take much to make an end of him. I should only have to give a little *squeeze* . . ."

This and all the other evidence of her temperament, her treatment of the Prince, her ambitions for herself, made the case against Sophie as having influenced the will look exceedingly strong. And behind it loomed the big question: suicide or murder? And if murder, at whose hand? Here, too, everything pointed in one direction. Outside the court the public had already made up its mind; she was lampooned and, whenever she appeared in the streets, mocked and openly insulted. In court, however, she continued to deny everything. No, she declared in her still imperfect French, she had no interest in money. "Honour" —perhaps she had found the word in a dictionary—meant everything to her.

When the hearing was over the judge spent much time and trouble in drawing up a meticulous report which would have made it impossible to avert the arrest of Sophie on a charge of murder. The report was sent to higher authority and for "reasons of state" promptly suppressed. The judge was forcibly retired and pensioned off. Presided over by another judge, the case was wound up, to the effect that there was no evidence of undue pressure from any quarter on the Prince when making his will and no evidence that he had died as the result of a crime.

So infamy triumphed. The King of France was saved from scandal, Sophie was saved from the guillotine. But she thought it prudent to absent herself from Paris for a time and went to England with her nephew. Soon after their return, the young man was suddenly taken ill and in a short while died in agony. Poisoned by his aunt? She had her reasons, it was said, for wanting him out of the way, having been told that he had made some ambiguous remarks about her in public. The cynically minded may be confirmed in this view by the piety she showed after his death. A simple grave in Paris would not do. With the body securely coffined she made the long trip back to England, accompanied it to Ryde, from Ryde trundled with it over rough tracks to St. Helens, and there buried her beloved nephew with a memorial at her own expense: "Erected as a mark of affection by his aunt, Madame La Baronne de Fouchères." "La Baronne" now, if you please!

Back in Paris, though, she found public opinion solidly against her and it was kept at boiling point by another court case to reverse the will which again, perhaps owing to royal influence, was unsuccessful. Meanwhile, anonymous pamphlets against her were appearing and she was treated everywhere as a contaminated object. "There is blood on her dress," said someone, seeing her at the opera. As for her relationship with Louis Philippe, she had served her purpose and the court was now firmly closed to her. The winkle had been picked and there was nothing left but the shell. But she had fought hard for her money and had no intention of relapsing into lonely poverty. As long as there was any life left to live, the idea of penance would have seemed ridiculous to her. So she turned her assets into liquid cash. The property of Saint Leu had been left to her; she now razed the château to the ground and sold the park for building plots. Then, wealthy but alone except for a niece whom she adopted, she travelled round Europe.

In 1837, Sophie Dawes returned to England, bought the estate of Bure Homage near Christchurch, built a mansion there and bought another house in Hyde Park Square. She had not forgotten her mother, who all these years had been living in Paris. The ninety-year-old woman was fetched back to England and entered a convent at Hammersmith, where she soon died. In the following year, Sophie, now very fat and coarse of feature, developed dropsy. She took this as a sign that it was now time to make her peace with heaven and by degrees gave away most of her huge fortune to charity. She died suddenly in December, 1840, of a heart attack and was buried in London, taking her secret with her, as she thought, to the grave. But some years later, documents came to light which proved that she had indeed planned the Prince's murder and that it had been carried out by her portly sergeant-lover who had suffocated the old man in bed.

So to the sports clubs and the geese of St. Helens we must add the scandalous Sophie Dawes. No one would pretend that she was a nice girl. But with its overtones of Nell Gwynn, Eliza Doolittle and Lady Macbeth her story is, to say the least, interesting. One might call it: From Brandy to Bourbon.

VIII

THE GOOD SIR JOHN

THERE is a kind of common denominator of loveliness to which we all pay lip service. Mountains, as long as one is not too close to them, can always be applauded. Rivers in unspoilt scenery are usually pretty good. Downs are invariably invigorating. There can never be much wrong with an open field. But that is about all one can say, with complete unanimity. Beyond that, as soon as we attempt to get at the heart of a scene and embark on closer description, it is our own heart that we lay bare, it is ourselves rather than the scenery that we start to analyse.

Consider two descriptions of Brading. One modern writer calls it "a one-horse place, straggling, scattered, somewhat dull at first glimpse". Another says that it is "full of charm, very picturesque, very curious". On a third writer the village itself appears to have made no impression at all and he starts straight in on the church. Where, in all this, is the truth about Brading? There seems to be a series of truths. It is successively one-horse, charming and completely beneath notice, depending on who is looking at it. The picture lies in the beholder's eye. It does indeed, for I must admit that, until a few years ago, I could not look at Brading with any sort of detachment. My view of the place was curdled by memories of a large ice-cream cornet given me there as a boy which promptly made me sick. Brading, the scene of agony and humiliation. Later, a more detached view showed me its charms and, later still, I came to realize that this whole area is dominated by a single remarkable family and my interest shifted to the dignified, spacious and well-proportioned church which stands at the top of the village. In that church, in their own chapel built late in the fifteenth century, where the sunlight piercing the stained-glass windows casts brilliant colours on a rich Turkey carpet and there is an unusually cheerful atmosphere, lie members of this family, the oldest in the island, whose ancestor Richard d'Oglandres came over with the Conqueror and helped William FitzOsbern to occupy the Isle of Wight.

Now these Oglanders are interesting for several reasons. They continued in an unbroken line from father to son for eight hundred years; since the Norman Conquest they have lived almost continually in the same place, at Nunwell, half a mile north-west of Brading; many of them have served the island faithfully as Deputy Lieutenants and Deputy Governors and they can claim amongst their ancestors Sir John Oglander (1585–1655), who has been called the most interesting and lovable personality that ever the island produced. This is a bold claim, but not an idle one, for we know much more about Sir John than about many living people, and from the best possible source, himself. He was a writer, or rather, even more valuable from the point of view of later generations, an inveterate scribbler, and from random notes and correspondence carefully preserved by him over many years emerges an authentic and endearing picture of this Jacobean gentleman, not a startling figure in any way, either in gifts or achievement, but a steady, warm-hearted, sensible man, imbued with a deep love for his family and his island home. That the islanders have taken him to their hearts is logical. The virtues he represents are island virtues bred of contentment, a fairly narrow horizon and an absence of gnawing ambition. In scale he seems to me exactly right as the symbol of a population which has never produced men of outstanding fame, but has always been busy about its own affairs, secure in the knowledge that the violent convulsions of the mainland have lapped but seldom engulfed its shores.

To appreciate Sir John, we need—and he would certainly wish us —to know something of his forebears, though the annals of the Oglander family prior to the seventeenth century are sketchy. FitzOsbern gave some hundreds of acres at Nunwell, at that time richly dotted with oaks, to Richard d'Oglandres. Within fifty years or so the family were styling themselves Doggelander and one of them was appointed chaplain to Richard de Redvers, Lord of the Wight. Thereafter, there was much intermarriage with local families, but in the surviving annals only two events are preserved from the next two hundred years: the repurchase of some Nunwell acres which had strayed to the Priory of Carisbrooke and the adventurous exploit of one John who, stifling perhaps under the blanket of peace that had lain for centuries on the island, went crusading in 1270 and safely returned. The family emblem of a stork was then embellished with three crosses crosslet. After this, semi-darkness again descends on the family fortunes. An Oglander helped to repel the French who landed uncomfortably close to Nunwell at St. Helens in 1340 and, after making an advantageous match with the daughter of a local magnate who was descended from Edward I, he is next heard of fighting at Crécy, where he was knighted on the field. In 1377, by an ironical twist of fortune, the family home was burnt down by the French during their big raid when they advanced as far as Carisbrooke. The French wars, due originally to the fact that the Norman conquerors had bequeathed a stake on the Continent to the English crown, continued to affect the family and long after a new Nunwell had been built two young Oglanders lost their lives on Sir Edward Wydville's ill-fated expedition in 1488 on behalf of the Duke of Brittany. In 1499, Henry VII, while inspecting the island defences, stayed a night at Nunwell.

Up to this point, the Oglanders seem to have fought when inclination or dury impelled them, but otherwise to have stayed at home and avoided public affairs. Now there is mention of one George becoming a student at Oxford and his elder brother Oliver being appointed Lieutenant-Governor of Guernsey. The lure of Nunwell and the island was still strong, however, and in 1522, after resigning his appointment, Oliver returned with his family, only to see the old home burnt to ashes in an accidental fire. There then took place the only permanent move which the family has ever made in nine hundred years—a move of half a mile to East Nunwell, where Oliver was able to buy another house. This, incidentally, is the house which still stands today, a charming mixture of Jacobean, Queen Anne and earlier styles, with an Oglander still in residence amid oaks dating back to the Conqueror and rolling parkland with distant glimpses of the Solent. When he died in 1536, Oliver was not the first to inhabit the Oglander chapel, but his table-tomb is still one of the finest, with the carved figures of himself, his wife and seven children kneeling in a row and all clasping large copies of the English Bible which was first issued in the year of his death.

Through stirring and dangerous times, Oliver's son George Oglander (1498–1566) and his son William (who was to be the father of the lovable Sir John) clung to Nunwell as their permanent home. As commander of the local defence forces, George helped to repel the

French invasion of 1545. In July 1588, William and his wife watched the Spanish Armada appear off the island and the ensuing sea fight which lasted for five hours. In one of his innumerable note-books Sir John later gave a pen-portrait of his grandfather. George had been a barrister, but had never practised. Apart from giving free legal assistance to his island friends and sitting on the Bench, he had spent much of his time in the field with his horses and hawks. But he was industrious like most of the Oglanders, no spendthrift and, according to his grandson, "one of the merriest, completest men that ever lived". Sir John also gave high praise to his own father, William, who was knighted by James I, a distinction which cost him £18, including £2 for the King's trumpeters and £1 for the porters at the King's gate. William had been well schooled at Winchester, but by the time he reached Balliol sporting instincts were dawning and his sole claim to fame at the university was to be the first youth "that had a birding and fowling piece in Oxford, which exercise of all others he affected". Back at Nunwell, aged twenty-one and finished with books, he horrified his family by marrying for love instead of the heiress singled out for him—and never regretted it. Very happily and contentedly the couple lived at Nunwell, producing children as fast as nature would allow. William always kept a hawk in summer and in winter liked to splash about in Brading Haven, pursuing wild-fowl with his piece —"a grave, fine-timbered man", his son informs us. "The best-natured man in the world. Well skilled in husbandry, charitable to the poor, very industrious. A better, more upright conscience never lived."

This is about all we know of the Oglanders until Sir John comes on the scene. But the fact of their survival at Nunwell for what was now over five hundred years, coupled with the preservation since the thirteenth century of documents relating to the family, shows that, at the least, they had always been careful people, imbued with a family tradition and strongly attached to their island home. In part, of course, their survival was due to the Solent. They had had no share in the murderous feuds of the Middle Ages. They had no call to summon their henchmen in the cause of the White Rose or the Red. But for the long line to survive at all through ages when death ruthlessly scythed the newly born argues a well-ordered domestic life as well as uncommon luck.

So when young John was born at Nunwell in 1585 he could count himself exceedingly fortunate. The family was prosperous, united and well thought of in the island. The population was flourishing, too. Looking back in later years he wrote that in his childhood both yeomen and gentry had plenty of money in their pockets and all the gentry were out of debt. "The market full, commodities venting themselves at most high prices, and men of war at the Cowes which gave great rates for our commodities, and exchanged other good ones with us. If you had anything to sell you should not have needed to have looked for a chapman, for you could not almost ask but have; all things were exported and imported at your heart's desire; your tenants rich, and a bargain could not stand at any rate. The State was well ordered; we had in a good manner wars with Spain and peace with France; and the Low Countrymen were our servants, not our masters . . ."

War with Spain, however, did not strike his parents as quite such a good arrangement and the mere sight of the Armada cruising off the island had been a traumatic experience for his mother, as it probably was for a great many other people. Her reaction, as the mother of a large family close to the likely landing-place of St. Helens, brings home to us the real possibility of islanders losing their lives and property in an invasion, whether or not the invaders were ultimately repelled. Not even the defeat of the Armada would comfort her and in 1590, at her insistence, William moved his family out of harm's way to Beaulieu Abbey which he leased from Lord Southampton, the patron of Shakespeare. There, with five sisters all older than himself, young John grew up, the darling of the household, but certainly robust enough to survive the petticoat influence. From time to time, William with his son went back to Nunwell to see that the old house was still standing and renew the joys of chilly sport in Brading Haven. Then, at an early age, there was Winchester for John, followed by Balliol and law at the Middle Temple. Meanwhile his mother had died and his father had married again. John's views on this find trenchant expression in a later notebook: "As no man living could have had a better wife than his first, so his last wife was clean contrary." This seems to have been the general opinion, for when William died in 1609 he was brought home from Sussex where he had been living and buried beside the mother of his family in yet another table-tomb, surmounted with an effigy, in the chapel at Brading where the sunlight streams in through the stained-glass windows and the Oglanders enjoy their long repose.

Married at twenty-one to a daughter of Sir George More, Lieutenant of the Tower, and sister-in-law of the poet John Donne, John now reigned as lord of Nunwell. As the son of a knight—there were only five at that time in the island—and soon to be knighted himself, with an income of £1,000 a year and a large estate, he was obviously destined for a leading role in island affairs. To his responsibilities, private and public, he brought a solid intelligence, a sense of duty and a burning interest in the welfare of his family and the island. Early in married life he began to suffer from troublesome symptoms which we can diagnose today as migraine and had to keep to his room periodically. There one of his first tasks was to sort the family correspondence and tie it up neatly with silver laces from his satin doublet —a fashion, he blandly noted, which later generations might be surprised at. Then he began to keep a diary, filling it with practically anything that came into his head and filing it away in a black box which also contained his own correspondence. On the lid he inscribed a solemn curse on anyone who opened it.

Assured now that the past would survive and the present be suitably documented, John Oglander set about managing his estates, learning husbandry and founding a family—all this in an island very different from the one we know today. The population was about 10,000, of which 87 were freeholders. Cowes was the chief port and Ryde only a tiny fishing village. Yarmouth was on the decline; Newport, with 2,000 people and a brand-new charter of incorporation from James I, in the ascendant. Newtown was about as supine as it is today. But all three places were boroughs and each returned two members to Parliament. Each parish supported its own poor and was supposed to maintain the roads in its vicinity. But this was so badly done that it was practically impossible for wheeled vehicles to move anywhere. Men travelled on horseback with their wives seated behind them on a pillion, and only John Oglander thought it worth keeping a coach, the second, as he proudly relates, that ever was in the island. We can imagine a contented and on the whole prosperous population, placid in outlook, not easily stirred to strife or, for that matter, to religious fervour, each little community living in isolation from its neighbour, the members meeting occasionally at Newport market, but otherwise only at the island defence musters which grew in unpopularity as the years of peace continued. A calm and spacious island, well stocked with game, happy so long as its governors did not become too autocratic, on good terms with the gentry, immune, as it seemed, from the quarrels of the mainland. Something of the peace of this Elysium crept into John Oglander's style when, years later, he wrote, as he so often did, for the benefit of his descendants: "Fear God as we did; marry a wife whom thou canst love; keep out of debt; see thy grounds well stocked; and thou mayest live as happily at Nunwell as any Prince in the world."

For many years, indeed, John and his wife Frances led a contented and uneventful existence and their interest for us lies in the small details he supplies of domestic life at that time. They had nine children, five boys and four girls, of whom seven survived infancy. From the boy's birth, all his hopes for the future were centred on his eldest son, George. The family lived well, but not extravagantly. Frances, he assures us, was "a most careful thriving wife, who was no spender, never wore a silk gown but for her credit when she went abroad in company and never to please herself". They kept three serving men and a footboy, total wages about £17 a year. Labourers on the estate would cost 4s. a week. Yet this country gentleman in the Isle of Wight, with as yet no outside commitments, could on his own reckoning only just get by on £1,000 a year. The fact was, I suspect, that thrift fought a losing battle in his mind with a desire to maintain the honour of the family. Honour demanded unstinting hospitality to his friends, tables groaning with mutton, beef, veal, rabbits, poultry, besides the sweetmeats beloved of Elizabethans and such exotic dishes as one mentioned in the family recipe book: "a roasted pig with a pudding in 's belly." Thrift called for a small saving each year, but this proved to be impossible. Besides entertainment, heavy expenditure was required on the estate and the house, which had been neglected during the time spent at Beaulieu. Appalled, the good Sir John—he was knighted in 1615—noted that in one year, in addition to the cost of food, he had spent £747 3s. 5d. "I *must* spend less, otherwise I shall be undone—but which way to begin I know not." Then, a habit of his when deeply moved, he pricked a finger and continued in red: "Sir John Oglander, with his own blood, his blood grieving at his great expense."

It is impossible not to think of this as intended for future generations, a solemn warning to the unthrifty, proof, long after he was gone, of their ancestor's emotion. And it was, indeed, one of his most curious and unusual characteristics that he lived as though the eyes of posterity were on him. He was very conscious of himself as a rounded and complete personality, a kind of lynch-pin in the Oglander line, a culmination of the past and an inspiration for the future. As a young man, he had written: "I so well affect my successors, and the advancement of the name of the Oglanders, that I hereby wish there may come some from me in time that may overtop and outgo me, both in wealth, wit, wisdom and honour." But no one ever did overtop him and he seems to have sensed that no one ever would. So advice pours from his pen, and always directed to his successors: "Be warned by me, learn from my experience . . ." He knew they would be curious about him, or perhaps felt merely that they ought to be, and he took care to satisfy their interest, compiling his own biographical notes, supplying explanations of his motives in important decisions and even, towards the end of his own life, writing a charming self-portrait beginning: "Wouldst thou feign see me, being dead so many years since . . . ?"

At the age of three, his eldest baby, George, came in for a long list of instructions entitled "Rules for a Happy Life" which he was "often to read and, reading seriously, to follow." In these, most of which were copied from Lord Burleigh's advice to his son, the infant was advised how to choose a wife, how to bring up his children and manage his affairs. The most revealing rule shows that advancement at that time was usually granted as a favour, not as a right. Nothing could be done without influential friends. "Be sure," George was told, "to keep some great man thy friend; but bother him not for trifles. Compliment him often; present him with many yet small gifts, and of little charge. If thou shouldst bestow any great gift, let it be some such thing as may be daily in his sight. Otherwise in this ambitious age thou shalt be like a hop without a pole."

Sir John, as it proved, already had his own hop-pole and some time after this he was appointed Lieutenant-Governor of Portsmouth by the Earl of Pembroke. But the duties were vexatious, the expenses were great and within three years he was back again at Nunwell, carefully recording his reasons for resigning the post, which boiled down to the fact that he preferred to be looking after his home and family. He had done well at Portsmouth and now, in his fortieth year, there was obviously scope for this capable man in the island. The Governor at this time was Lord Conway, a weak though amiable courtier who never even bothered to cross the Solent. Of his two deputies on the spot, one was an old man of over eighty who in Sir John's opinion was no longer sane, and the other, Sir Edward Dennys, "a very honest man and stout", but a tedious gasbag. In 1624, to his undoubted delight, Sir John was appointed to make a triumvirate with these gentlemen, in other words in practice given sole control of the island. He recorded later, with that curious double vision which gave him such magisterial detachment: "God send the Island never a worse for his painstaking to administer justice uprightly to everyone; and for the appeasing and ending of difference and debates between neighbour and neighbour." We can take this as true, for, again by his own account, he was very jealous of his good reputation and he certainly loved the island and its people.

One can imagine that this buoyant and honest knight exactly suited the times. There was an air of confidence throughout the island and a belief that the dangerous days were past. In the valleys, well sheltered from the wind, stone manor houses were springing up. On summer Saturdays and twice during the week the big landowners met on St. George's Down to play bowls and drink together, or else they dined in Newport and eyed the pretty girls. And pretty they were, we have Sir John's word for it: "As it is an honour for our island to have neither fox nor Papist in it, so it is an imputation or tax that is laid on it, never or seldom to be guilty of breeding a handsome woman or horse. I can say that no part of England, the quantity considered, hath produced more exquisite in either species than this island." Thus spoke the local patriot.

As Deputy Governor (or Lieutenant as he called it, thinking that the name Governor smacked too much of tyranny), Sir John was not too engrossed in business to take part in these festivities. The fun was simple and boisterous. Of his great friend Sir Richard Worsley of Appuldurcombe we are told: "He delighted much in flinging of cushions at one another's heads, only in sport and for exercise; until that with a cushion at Gatcombe I was like to put forth his eye." At a christening near Ashey Sir John writes of "the greatest drinking and uncivil mirth that ever I knew". A hundred musketeers had been provided, fifty in the garden and fifty in the courtyard of the house, and as each health was drunk they shot off their pieces into the parlour doors, "so that we drank as much smoke as wine". All this was very good, but Sir John was no friend of drunkenness. With majestic objectivity he wrote of himself: "Of all vices he hated drunkenness; yet he would play the good fellow and would not much refrain from drinking two or three healths." So he lived up to the advice given to his son: "Banish swinish drunkenness from thy house. . . . I have never heard praise ascribed to a drunkard but the well-bearing of his liquor, which is a better commendation for a brewer's horse than a gentleman."

As *de facto* Governor (with sporadic help from the loquacious Sir Edward Dennys), Sir John was soon embroiled, however, in heavy duties and troubles. For a month the absent Lord Conway saddled him with one Mr. Reede who after copious entertainment at Nunwell took back with him to London a report on the island defences. This showed that about two out of every three men served in the "Home Guard", armed with muskets, halberds or pikes. But some three hundred of them possessed no weapons at all. This had to be remedied, for it was an age when England took a keen interest in the Protestant cause on the Continent and war with Spain or France might break out at any time. The islanders' growing confidence was easily shattered and such possibilities made them jittery. Already, a few years before, there had been panic in the East Wight when some Hamburg merchant ships had anchored at St. Helens and their crews were rumoured to be invading the island. At Nunwell, Sir John had leapt on a horse and cantered towards the trouble. At Brading the terrified yokels had told him that five hundred men were ashore. Nearer St. Helens the figure had grown to a thousand and the people there were streaming inland, including one old man of eighty-nine, bed-ridden for five years, who covered three miles. On reaching the coast Sir John found not a soul. But meanwhile, a servant of his had fired the Nunwell beacon, the alarm had spread to Portsmouth, and from Portsmouth fast messengers set off to inform King James. As a result, the fleet was ordered out to succour the Isle of Wight, now reported to be in enemy hands.

All that was in times of peace, but after the accession of Charles I war really came, first with Spain and then with France. Soon further vexations descended on Sir John. There was a royal demand for money, a forced loan to be raised from the island gentry under a Privy Seal. He did his best to distribute the loan fairly, but he and Sir Edward incurred much ill will. Then he was ordered to scrape together the riff-raff of the island, not able-bodied persons who were reserved for the militia, but "fugitives and such as are of little or no use" for service in the navy. Fifteen Lords of the Council, each one of them signing the letter, then urgently abjured the Deputy Governors to put the island forts in a fit state of repair. And then, the last straw, it was announced that "overners", foreign troops virtually, from the mainland were to be billeted in the island prior to service overseas. The English aim was to occupy the Ile de Rhé as an advanced base for the relief of La Rochelle, maritime stronghold of the Huguenots which Cardinal Richelieu was determined to reduce. An elaborate expedition was planned under the showy but incompetent Duke of Buckingham and these overners, an entire regiment of Englishmen, were to play a part in the attack. Sir John hurried to London in an attempt to avert their arrival, but was unsuccessful and in May, 1627, they came, a thousand strong. From the lack of stringent comment in his notebooks one can deduce that they behaved themselves. At any rate, there was no shortage of food and the lodging problem was solved by dispersing single companies to each of the larger villages. Their presence may even have been welcome, for while these troops were in the island there was another invasion scare which shows clearly how, in those days of poor intelligence, the whole country could be at the mercy of rumour. On 30th May, the captain of a small warship off the south coast of the island spotted a fleet of twenty-two sail which he took to be Spanish. Landing as quickly as he could he sent a letter to Sir Edward Dennys. Sir Edward despatched it to Portsmouth. Portsmouth rose in arms. By two o'clock that same night the news was in London—of sixty Spanish ships making for Portsmouth. Next morning, the Duke of Buckingham went to Dover to see to the safety of the castle and order the King's navy, then in the Downs, to contact the enemy. But no enemy could be found, only a number of Dutch ships laden with salt.

No sooner was the scare over than august personages descended on the island, first, King Charles in person to inspect the billeted regiment. Out came the Nunwell coach. Forty horses and as many gentlemen were mustered and Sir John met his sovereign at Ryde. The regiment was paraded on Arreton Down. On the way there he had plenty of time to discuss various island problems with the King—more ammunition, more forts, warships to be stationed permanently at Portsmouth —and we can imagine that he pressed his suit with vigour. The King was affable, conceded everything, but that night Sir John noted in his diary: "So much promised, and how happy we if performed . . ."

On returning to the mainland, the King seems to have told the

The famous and the infamous: Lord Tennyson and Sophie Dawes
(overleaf) Sheat Manor

absentee Governor, Lord Conway, that after two years of office it would be as well to visit the island. At any rate, it was not long before his Lordship arrived. Sir John did his best. At Newport one of the grammar school scholars delivered a Latin oration; the mayor offered cakes and wine; there was a general defence muster; "ye companye of Bwoyes", a kind of island cadet force, skirmished before him and fired off the ordnance at Carisbrooke; provisions flowed in from the gentry to accompany him on his travels, and he was lavishly entertained at Nunwell. All this, like the King, he requited with affability and large promises regarding the needs of the island. The good Frances and her daughters at Nunwell were smothered with flowery compliments; their serving women also. But again Sir John was not deceived. Lord Conway he wrote off as "old, unwieldy and very sickly; neither fit for employment or command". He spoke very well to all, but his words were better than his performance—in short, "a mere verbal man".

So the island carried on as best it could, with benevolence from London, but not much else. The English soldiers stayed only a month and as their billeting, by some miracle, was paid for, Sir John made no complaint. By contrast with the Scotsmen that now arrived, they were angels incarnate. "Ye Scottish Regyment" fills quite a few pages in the Oglander notebooks. It came as reinforcement for the La Rochelle expedition, but when this ended in failure it stayed for exactly a year until a second enterprise could be mounted which failed as dismally as the first. Meanwhile, 1,500 Highlanders, in the Deputy Governor's opinion "as barbarous in their nature as their clothes", kicked their heels in the island, where they had been sent as a safeguard against desertion. This was indeed a serious affliction. No money was forthcoming for the luckless householders who fed and housed them, there was nothing for them to do and their officers, being inexperienced, were unable to control them. Yet it was they who possessed the sole powers of punishment. One can imagine the consequences: "murders, rapes, robberies, burglaries, getting of bastards (70!), and almost the undoing of the whole island." Before long there was a veritable reign of terror. Few of the malefactors could be brought to book and as the toll of crime mounted the Scotsmen became more truculent and clung more closely together. Appeals to the Council in London were dismissed with fair words. When two islanders were murdered in June 1628, a local resident who wrote to Lord Conway begged him

Godshill (overleaf)
Ventnor

not to reveal his name in case of reprisals. Not even a second visit from the King achieved much improvement. Taxed by Sir John for billeting money and with a long list of complaints, he was artfully evasive: "He took me by the hand and held me a long time riding together, saying he was bound to us all for our patience and well usage of the Scotsmen and commanded me to thank the whole island in his name . . ."

With this the island had to be content. But soon after the King's visit the Scotsmen departed on the second expedition to La Rochelle and Sir John was left, simmering with rage, to record in his diary: "The greatest error that ever our Island committed was the admitting of the Scottish Regiment. For prevention of the like, or any in this kind hereafter, I would wish my countrymen, seeing the billeting of soldiers is contrary to the law and liberty of freemen, never to suffer any more at any time to come into the Island; but rather with the danger of their lives to hinder them at the landing." These are strange words to come from a Deputy Governor and ardent Royalist, but Sir John was devoted to what he called "our ancient island" and he must have felt deeply aggrieved that such horrors could occur, and go unpunished, during his tenure of office. It was a long time before his wrath cooled and periodically drastic expressions about the Scots kept bubbling up in his notes: "a miserable oppression . . . an unsupportable trouble and misery . . . an Egyptian thraldom . . . since the Danish slavery never were these islanders so oppressed . . ."

One presumes, however, though Sir John does not mention it, that there was a redeeming feature about the Egyptian thraldom, namely that the oppressors were soldiers and could, if need be, have defended the island against a foreign invader. At any rate, when they left the islanders seem suddenly to have felt the draught and January, 1629, found Sir John in London with a delegation of gentlemen seeking money from the King for a somewhat extraordinary scheme. If an invader conquered the East Wight, where he would be most likely to land, the idea was that the entire population should withdraw to the West and turn Freshwater into an island by breaking through the narrow strip of land which separates the source of the Yar from the sea. In Freshwater the common folk with their cattle and such troops as had managed to escape the foe would take up their abode, while Yarmouth would be converted into an island on its own, with drawbridges and half-moons, to accommodate "the better sort of people".

To achieve this desirable object £500 would be needed, a lot of money in those days. But that was not all. It was necessary to build new island forts and repair existing ones. That would cost another £2,500. No chicken-feed!

It is amusing, reading between the lines of Sir John's account, to see how the King and his advisers dealt with this project. One can imagine the worthy knight and his friends, hot from the island, obsessed with their schemes and propounding them in inordinate detail. How dismayed they would have been if they had seen into the royal mind! Their visit coincided with the start of Charles's attempt to rule without Parliament, in other words without money except what he could scrape together by questionable devices. Far from his mind was continued war with France or indeed with anyone. He saw clearly that he, his court and the whole executive would have to live on the smallest scale. And here were these country bumpkins asking for a cool £3,000 for their last-ditch defence against enemies with whom the King was determined to be friends. So he was very bland. He told them their fears were groundless, he was "on very good terms with his brother of France". Then he referred them to the Council of War. The Councillors gave the gentlemen many good words, but were slightly mocking. The islanders were too fearful, they said. Not at all, replied Sir John, merely circumspect. With rumours of great preparations in France they could do no less than make their weakness known to the Council. After all, the loss of the island would be serious for the whole kingdom. "We are told," broke in someone, "that you have removed your wives, children and goods. Is that true?" "Upon my life and reputation," retorted Sir John, "when I came out of the island there was not as much as a silver spoon removed." Then he neatly turned the gibe. "But if Your Lordships do not assist us in our just suit, then certainly our wives and children will not stay." The Councillors beat a retreat. They were glad to hear, they said, that their information was incorrect. Then they dismissed the suppliants "till another day".

But Sir John had not shot his bolt. He now descended on his old friend the Earl of Pembroke, former Governor of Portsmouth, and Richard Weston, Lord Treasurer, two years later to be made Governor of the island. This was the same Lord Weston who at that precise time was being made the subject of a solemn remonstrance in the House of Commons for his alleged Papist, if not Jesuit sympathies and his illegal exaction of taxes. A resourceful man, obviously, in money matters and a very good one to consult—so long as the King sat firmly on the neck of Parliament. To these gentlemen and the frothy Lord Conway, Sir John once again unpacked his scheme, coupled with a request for billet money for the Scots, over £8,000, no less, a grand total, with the other demands, which today would amount to £222,000. How to placate this ruddy-faced knight, with his big moustaches and bigger ideas? Weston may well have pondered. He decided to play for time. "You shall have some money forthwith," he said, "and we will send you a good engineer to plan the construction of your forts, and we will pay him out of the Exchequer. As for the £8,000, you shall have it as soon as His Majesty can possibly pay." Then Sir John asked for some warships to be stationed about the island until it was fortified. That, too, was conceded. "And we should like our islanders to command them." Very well, agreed. . . . "And I should like to leave this gentleman here, Sir Bevis Thelwell, behind, to keep in touch with you." Sir John does not record the answer, but Sir Bevis stayed.

For two years, however, practically no money seems to have been forthcoming. Meanwhile, back in the island, Sir John shepherded his growing family. From his correspondence we gather that they were all coming along nicely. The fifteen-year-old Ann, his eldest daughter, was the apple of his eye: "Famous far and near for her handsomeness", he tells us. "As handsome a gentlewoman as ever this Isle bred, and the handsomest that ever came out of the family of the Oglanders." Sir John was fond of driving home his points. But all hopes for the future rested on George, now twenty and at the Middle Temple studying law, at least supposed to be studying. "Catch time by the forelock", abjured his father, not at all reassured by letters blabbing of drinking bouts which would entail "some necessary expense" on sack posset and burnt wine, an expense which he, of course, was expected to meet. George had also incurred displeasure for allowing a wealthy though slightly deformed heiress to slip through his fingers and then falling in love with a penniless beauty. Massive screeds flew up from Nunwell signed "your father, careful of your good", though the advice they contained was curiously mild. It was clear that Sir John did not want a hideous daughter-in-law, however opulent; on the other hand, beauty in rags would do no good to the Oglanders. So the core of his advice was confined to the impeccable generalization that all good portions were not inseparably tied to ill faces. In other words, the search much be continued, with hope and circumspection.

As yet, the younger sons were giving no trouble. Spaced like the rungs of a ladder, aged eighteen and sixteen, they were forging ahead towards the Law and the Church. At fourteen, another boy, Richard, was apprenticed to a silk mercer in London. "Be sure", recorded the sensible father, "to give all thy sons a vocation. Keep not thy children idly at home to be bird catchers or dog drivers, but be sure to settle them in a course of life, lest the name of gentry maketh them too high for it, and in the end bringeth them to beggary." But in 1629, small-pox, then ravaging the island and particularly the capital, swept the tail from the hopeful procession, killing the youngest girl and boy, then scarcely out of the nursery. This calamity also found record in the notebooks, Sir John finding some consolation in the fact that his children, who had been staying in Chichester when they died, were buried "among ye kings" in the Cathedral.

It was now perhaps, when the risk of infection was so great that many villages refused to admit people from Newport and the wisest course was to stay at home, that Sir John took time off from his duties to write up his voluminous notes. In earlier years he had explored the island from end to end, visiting the churches, examining the memorials and recording the inscriptions, digging for bones in ancient burial mounds, poking about among the ruins of Quarr to trace the founda-tions of the Abbey. The fruits of this research were now written down in a flowery hand upon foolscap, together with the genealogies, inter-spersed with stringent comment, of the island families. These Sir John firmly sorted into the sheep and the goats. Those gentlemen who built up their estates and were good family men received generous praise. The supreme tribute was to be called "my good friend". But if the family was an ancient one the severest standards were applied. For the spendthrift sons of diligent fathers who squandered their in-heritance he had nothing but contempt. On the other hand, wealth unallied to virtue never impressed him. Heavy thunder descended on a family named Gard, who "now begin to grow rich in our island", but, as Sir John informs his descendants, by very questionable means. The father, who came to the island from Normandy in Queen Eliza-beth's reign, "was a notable sly fellow, dishonest and given to filching; he brought some tricks out of France with him. *Vide*, he would steal a cow, and putting a loaf of bread hot out of the oven on her horns, make them so supple that they would turn any way he pleased, so as to disfigure the beast that the owner might not know her again." The son of this old bandit, named Richard, was "as crafty a knave as any (except his brother) in the whole country". He had posed as an attorney, stirred up lawsuits and enriched himself at the expense of warring neighbours. Sir John was convinced that he and his better qualified brethren had ruined the island. One attorney he knew had issued no less than three hundred writs. The result had been strife, enmity and endless trips to London or Winchester to plead in the courts. This was a sorry contrast with the later days of Elizabeth when the people had lived securely and quietly, seldom leaving the island and, when they did, making their wills, supposing a journey to London to be the equivalent of an East India voyage. In those days, no lawyers were allowed to cross the Solent. One who tried to settle in the island was hunted out on the orders of Sir George Carey with a pound of lighted candles hanging at his breeches and bells about his legs. How Sir John wished that as Deputy Governor he could mete out the same treatment. But, alas, times had clean altered. As he wrote, the Gards were still flourishing, though the old man was long since dead, buried, at his request, in a lead coffin to prevent physical decay only two feet down in the porch of Godshill church so that at the resurrection he could get a good start on the rest of humanity for another life of stealing cows. Not that Sir John despised him for his humble origin. Mr. Emanuel Badd, a poor man's son and once apprenticed to a shoemaker in Newport, had his deepest respect. In his youth he had married a girl with a fat dowry who had then died, and this had happened to him several times. "By God's blessing," wrote Sir John, "and the loss of five wives he grew very rich", and became High Sheriff of Hampshire, "and was a very honest man and a very good friend of mine."

But Sir John's comments were mostly reserved for more notable persons, including Lord Conway, who died in 1631. The islanders had never taken kindly to their absentee Governor, blaming him (wrongly) for the billeting of the Scottish Regiment and (rightly) for failure to procure money for defence. But in retrospect Sir John had been well enough pleased. Lord Conway had been an excellent father and husband, and that excused much else. He had also left the effective government to Sir John. So when the islanders, with churlish glee, consoled themselves for the trials of daily life by saying: "But my Lord Conway is dead", he reminded them of Aesop's fable of the frogs, implying that they might have fared worse.

No doubt at the back of every islander's mind hovered a picture of the ideal Governor, a lavish entertainer, a worthy figure-head, someone with good connections who would keep the money pouring in, and when a new one was appointed, all, with renewed hope, helped to roll out the red carpet. This time, it was Richard Weston, now Earl of Portland. He received the traditional treatment. Sir John met him at Ryde where he landed with no less than three hundred companions. The whole party was then led over Brading Down to Newport where a house had been reserved for the Governor stacked with provisions: hogsheads of sack, claret and white wine, a fat ox, fish of all sorts, gulls, rabbits, pigeons, pheasants, partridges and chickens. On the doorstep waited a scholar with a Latin oration. The ordnance was shot off at Carisbrooke, the small boys skirmished, and when His Lordship made a quick tour of the island all the villages rang their bells and the people waved and shouted. With all this, and particularly the good fare, the Governor was highly delighted. Out from his baggage came £1,000 in gold towards the billeting of the Scottish Regiment, with promises (slowly fulfilled) of more to come. When he left after three days to the booming of guns from Cowes, Sir John hurried back to his notes and wrote with a contented sigh: "Never was any Captain of the Island braver entertained, or nobler used and respected—we live in expectation of the like from him."

But within three years Richard Weston was dead and his son Jerome, 2nd Earl of Portland, reigned in his stead. It was a rule so shameful that Sir John's quivering pen could scarce record the facts. With his boon companion, Colonel (later Lord) Goring, the Governor, after heavy bouts in Portsmouth "where they drank and shot, shot and drank till they were scarce *compos mentis*, came into the island where they did the like. I may truly say that in the space of six days there was never so much powder fired, except against an enemy. Tuesday, 2nd September, 1639, they all dined at Sandam Fort where they were all mad, at every health tearing of each other's bands and shirts in so much as linen was very hard to be found amongst them . . ." Then the revellers lurched on to Newport, where Goring climbed the gibbet and from the top of the ladder delivered an oration to the scandalized citizens, recanting his crimes and urging them to be warned by his example. From this point, Sir John's writing becomes more ragged, with numerous blots: ". . . and the Friday, my Lord went out of the country to Portsmouth . . . the powder that was shot off here and at Portsmouth in the space of eight days was better worth than £300 . . ."

But worse calamities loomed than a drunken Governor and at the time this was written Sir John had suffered a grievous personal blow. In 1632, his eldest son George, then aged twenty-three, had died suddenly of smallpox when on holiday in France. His mother had had a premonition that she would never see him again, but the indulgent father had consented to the trip, believing that it would do his son good. Now all his hopes were buried in an anonymous grave on foreign soil. No harsher stroke of fate, more insulting to human feeling, could be imagined, and from those far-off days a faded scrawl comes down to us as poignant testimony of his grief: "With my tears instead of ink I write these lines . . ."

The sorrow of bereavement did not, however, prevent him from keeping a close eye on his other sons, admonishing them when reports of over-indulgence in food and drink reached his ears and searching anxiously for suitable wives. They seem to have lived in healthy awe of him, but their letters also reveal affection and it speaks much for his kindness of heart that they all ultimately married girls of their own choice, just as he had done.

But while the family marched forward, united under its ever-thoughtful, ever-watchful head, fate was laying a trap. Once already he had incurred ill-will among the island gentry for raising a forced loan on behalf of the King. Now, in 1637, much against his wishes he was appointed High Sheriff of Hampshire. His chief objection was that he did not want to leave the island and the concession was made that he could continue to live at Nunwell, going to the mainland only for Assizes Week. His main task, in the unlooked-for appointment, was to assess and levy Ship Money, the highly unpopular tax revived two years before by Charles's ingenious lawyers on a precedent dating back to the times of Alfred the Great. The principle had then been established that all parts of the kingdom, inland as well as coastal areas, should contribute to the upkeep of the fleet. But in course of time it had been allowed to lapse, so that in living memory only counties by the sea had paid for the ships which defended all, excluding, for some reason, the Isle of Wight. Now, to their fury, the King was demanding contributions from Warwickshire squires, Derbyshire parsons, and the island gentry. As High Sheriff, Sir John was responsible for collecting the money and he flung himself into the task with strict fairness, but also with loyal zeal. He found himself prodding a hornets' nest. The islanders argued and pleaded with him and finally threatened social ostracism. All to no avail. To Mr. Worsley of Gatcombe, his honoured friend, he wrote: "As you are a gentleman whom I love and respect, so I desire you not to force me to distrain your goods for His Majesty's Ship Monies. I should be very loth to do it to any, especially to yourself. But as the monies must be paid, so there is little reason that I should pay them out of my own purse . . ."

Good sense, at the time, but the Civil War was at hand and on its outbreak Sir John was already an unpopular figure, a marked and uncompromising Royalist. We have seen in an earlier chapter how the island gentry pursued the wise but unheroic course of trimming their sails to the parliamentary wind, and when Portsmouth with half the fleet fell to the Roundheads early in the war the island was already in the grip of the new régime. But as Deputy Governor Sir John fulfilled to the last his duty to the King and his responsibilities for maintaining order in the island. A loyal declaration which he drew up before the outbreak of the war was signed by some, but not all of the gentry. After the outbreak he intervened repeatedly to prevent arbitrary arrests, called on the captains of parliamentary ships to discipline their crews which had been landed in the island to intimidate the populace and took no action to enforce a decree which ordered the wife of the deposed Governor, Lord Portland, to leave the island within two days. All this, coupled with indiscreet remarks about the "theft" of the King's ships, swiftly led to his own deposition and arrest. It cannot have been unexpected. Earlier in that year of 1643, censorious remarks had been passed in the House of Commons on "the demeanour and carriage of one Oglander in the Isle of Wight" and when in June a party of horsemen with a warrant banged on the door of Nunwell, the event was viewed by him with splendid detachment. This was another milestone in the Oglander story, by no means inglorious, and as proof to later generations of his devotion to the royal cause he begged the piece of paper from his captors, later adding it to the family file and proudly inscribing it: "My Warrant."

The warrant, signed by members of the Committee of Safety in London, ordered Sir John to be brought to the capital "to answer such matters as shall be objected to him", and with him went a letter from the man who had stepped into his shoes as Deputy Governor, a rancorous Colonel Carne of obscure origins who made £8,000 for himself out of the island in five years. "I have sent up Sir John Oglander," he wrote, "and sufficient matter to keep him awhile by the leg. Peradventure the place will be the better for his absence, and some of the clergy (God willing) shall soon follow him."

In London, Sir John was put under open arrest, fined £1,000 and after two months sent home. His answers to the Committee must have been astute, for it had been well primed with information against him, raked up, after his thirty-six years' service to the island, by former friends. But the island itself was now ruled by a Committee of Safety which included such competent persons as a former pedlar of Newport, an apothecary, a baker and two farmers. No sooner had he returned than they informed him, through the ignoble Carne, that he was required to contribute £50 for the relief of the Commonwealth "before Saturday next". Then he was summoned to Carisbrooke, ostensibly to give Carne his advice, where he found the other island gentlemen assembled. They were discussing whether troops from the island should be sent to Southampton, allegedly in fear of a Royalist attack. Of course, everyone said yes, and then looked at Sir John. . . . What could he say? To send the island militia overseas was a thing which in all history had never been done. But he knew that to say no would be both useless and highly dangerous. So, with the other men, he signed a document promising his help in mustering the militia if required—and then went home to inform posterity that he had been forced to this step and was none the less a faithful servant of His Majesty.

Within ten days he was arrested again, again on orders from London, and this time it was two and a half years, spent partly on bail and partly as a prisoner, before he was fined once more and allowed to go home. By then his wife had died, the King had been defeated and the islanders were heartily longing for an end to faction and the baker-apothecary rule. In former times, so old men told them, the island was renowned for the strong affection that bound the inhabitants to the gentry. But now all ties were dissolved, informers were rife, sacrilege was held as a virtue, life was cheap and brother was divided against brother. To Sir John, when he got back, the island seemed a miserable, melancholy, dejected place, "no company, no resort, no neighbours seeing one another. Would I could write, or that I could be permitted to write the history of these times . . ."

His gloom was further increased by the arrival of King Charles in the island. To him the choice seemed inexplicable. There would be no safety there for his person and certainly no opportunity to arrange his escape. After the King's execution he recorded as a fact, not as his opinion, that Hammond had been appointed Governor purposely to be the royal keeper. The flight from Hampton Court had been provoked by stories that the Levellers were intending to kill the King, and when Charles reached Tichfield it was Hammond who persuaded him to come to the island. This may be true, for as long as Charles was at Carisbrooke Sir John saw him once a week and the story may have come from his own lips. There is another fact which adds strength to Sir John's assertion. Two days after Charles landed, he unexpectedly invited himself to Nunwell for the night, and in the circumstances this can only have been for one purpose: to sound his loyal adherent about the island situation and decide what further action to take. In this context Charles must have revealed why he had come at all; either Hammond had invited him with promises of help, or he had come voluntarily in expectation of support. Of the visit Sir John, who had learnt extreme caution by now, merely records: "In the Parlour Chamber I had some speech with him which I shall forbear to discover."

The story of King Charles in the island has already been told and no further light is shed on it by Sir John, normally so loquacious, but here discreet for obvious reasons. Did he take part in organizing any of the King's attempts to escape? Did he give his advice? Were the Nunwell horses held ready, perhaps, for a midnight dash with a royal rider to St. Helens? We do not know. His papers are silent on the Carisbrooke imprisonment, the abduction to Hurst Castle, and the terrible scene in Whitehall. The summer of 1649, when the execution was long past, finds him eagerly listening by correspondence to his daughter Ann, now happily married and living on the mainland, who has a tale to tell about a blind child miraculously cured by a handkerchief dipped in the King's blood. In the following year he entertained at Nunwell the young Duke of Gloucester, recently sent with his sister, Princess Elizabeth, for safe-keeping to Carisbrooke. Two months later, the ageing widower was again arrested for reasons unknown, again sent to London and released after a few months on payment of yet another fine.

He now came back to Nunwell and never left it. Politics were over and with his son George, his wife and his royal master all dead the days of his contentment were past. Under the Protectorate he and his whole family had to live cautiously, minding their every step. But there was one great consolation. His son and heir William was proving a capable manager of the estates, and William had an only son, Jack. With luck, the Oglander line which had survived from father to son for five hundred years would continue. So Sir John composed himself for the end with the thought that all the struggles and the heartbreak had not been in vain, and in his simple faith no doubt he saw the Oglanders well established in two realms, on earth and in heaven. There he would meet his wife and beloved son again, and from there he would watch over the family as it trod forward through the centuries.

"Fear God as we did; marry a wife whom thou canst love . . ." All that was safely recorded, together with practical advice on farm management, recipes for food, terrifying prescriptions for treating the common ailments. The letters were tied up with his silver points. The notebooks lay securely in the black leather box. There was only one thing left to do, before handing over the reins: supply a description of himself. So the old man took up his pen and wrote in his flowery hand: "Conceive thou sawest an aged, somewhat corpulent man, of middle stature, with a white beard and big moustaches, riding in black or some sad-coloured clothes over the downs to take the air, morning and evening, to see there his fatting cattle, on a handsome middling black horse, his hair grey and his complexion very sanguine. So I conceive myself, and so mayest thou, too, if thou hast any desire."

Just such a corpulent knight, with red face and flowing moustaches, Sir John had found in painted wood some years before in a London antique shop. The figure represented, in fact, a crusader in plate armour, lying on his side with a rather blank expression like a surfeited guest at a Roman banquet. This figure was brought back to Nunwell and when he died in 1655 Sir John left instructions for it to be placed on top of his tomb. So in the Oglander chapel, where the sunlight streaming through the windows casts bright pools on the Turkey carpet, Sir John rests, travestied at his own desire by this curious effigy, but loved and respected, as they assure us, by the Oglanders of today as he has been by all his descendants. And I fancy they can almost hear his voice as he writes for them with his pride in the family and also his deep sense of duty: "We have kept this spot of ground these five hundred years from father to son, and I pray God thou beest not the last, nor see that scattered which so many have taken care to gain for thee."

IX

RAIL AND SAIL

THE early history of Ryde is exceedingly scanty. Known in Norman times as La Riche or La Rye, it was destroyed by the French in the time of Richard II. For centuries it remained a tiny fishing village, distinguished only by the fact that ships called here from the mainland. In 1750 it consisted of two detached hamlets, one nestling above the other amid elm trees, and in 1753 Henry Fielding, on his way to die in Lisbon, recorded that he was carried ashore from his ship between two stalwart sailors across the mud-flats which today still dankly extend by the shore at low tide. In his time the wherries came in as far as they could through the shallow water, then the passengers were transferred to a horse-drawn cart or sedan chairs or the waiting arms of local fishermen and once ashore they found conditions extremely primitive. The reputation of the place was not improved by a disaster which occurred in 1782. In the summer of that year Britain's largest warship, the *Royal George*, suddenly heeled over and sank in Spithead. Of the eight hundred people who were drowned, including most of the crew with their wives and sweethearts who had come to see them off, scores were washed ashore at Ryde and given crude burial in waste land now occupied by the three-and-a-half-acre boating lake. "When Kempenfelt went down with twice four hundred men", sang the poet Cowper, and well into Victoria's reign visitors listened wide-eyed to local labourers who told them that when digging the foundations of houses they had come across bones, nothing but bones.

But by then, Ryde was well on the road to prosperity. The pier, the second longest in Britain, had bridged the mud. Theatres, libraries and churches had shot up; the two hamlets were now fused into one. And Ryde was already acquiring the reputation, which it still possesses, of being the most convenient base from which to view the island. In 1800, the population was about 1,000. Fifty years later it had multiplied ten times. Today it is considerably in excess of 20,000 and the town is the best shopping centre in the island, in style and amenities the nearest approach to a large-scale mainland pleasure resort, with elegant hotels, a sweeping esplanade, riotous flowers, plenty of space. "Bright, bracing and beautiful", claims the glossy hand-out, and proceeds to list twenty separate ways of amusing yourself, not including the famous boating lake where kiddies weave to and fro over the buried bones.

But Ryde has a problem, and this is how to disperse the flood of visitors who stream in through this main sluice-gate to the island. At summer weekends, ferries arrive and depart every fifteen minutes, carrying 1,300 people at a time, with another 2,000 per day arriving by hovercraft. On Saturdays, before the Beeching axe was wielded in the 1960s, 123 trains and innumerable coaches helped to take them away. But the Saturday of August Bank Holiday was always liable to provoke a bottle-neck and on one of those days since the war 21,000 people had to be dispersed. Now, with the sole remaining island railway (using electric trains from the London Underground) linking Ryde to Sandown and Shanklin only and already congested, the problem would become unmanageable if the County Council took no further steps to speed dispersal.

When the island railways were swept away except for that one short stretch no one rejoiced, for they had charm and character. Now the last tank-engine, with its Westinghouse brake-pump going "fish-pish" beside the boiler, has nosed into Newport station, the last train has plunged into Ventor through the tunnel under St. Boniface Down (which the local people once vigorously opposed because they thought the northern blast would ruin the climate of their paradise), and the porter there has swung his hand-bell for the last time, to warn would-be travellers that the train is due to leave immediately and will only wait five minutes.

With many others, the little station of St. Lawrence, tucked into the hillside like a minor frolic of the mad King Ludwig of Bavaria, is closed and has a notice-board giving its history as an island antiquity, and lovers walk along the torn-up track that once linked Yarmouth to Freshwater. All this is sad because apart from their usefulness the island railways had charm and character, the trains hustled about in idyllic scenery and small boys could justly dream of driving them after attaching a label: not a toy.

Railways came late to the island, over twenty years after the London-

Southampton line had been opened and when the direct link between Waterloo and Portsmouth had been in operation for some time. The thought of trains clattering over the landscape aroused widespread dismay. Local magnates would have none of them and did their best to prevent the development by refusing to sell land. Humbler folk were torn between the desire to attract more tourists and the fear of driving them away. Writers, of whom an eager throng were pouring out books and guides on the island, most of them cribbing from each other, varied between caution and outright terror. Notably one Mr. Davenport Adams, who sustained a note of poetic frenzy throughout an immense tome and could hardly describe a gasworks without peopling it with elves and fawns, wrote feelingly: "The winds that roam through the island dells and storm across the island hills, that stir the white crests of the Solent or agitate into anger the broad waters of the Channel bear no loud whistle, nor whirr of ceaseless wheels, to scare the Naiad from her haunts or the Oread from her groves. May it ever be so!" From which we gather that Mr. Adams was against trains.

But local promoters, eyeing the fabulous profits made from railways on the mainland, were busy and they first settled on a safe, not too ambitious project promising a steady return from passenger traffic. This was for a line of only four and a half miles between Cowes and Newport. It was opened in 1862 amid a noticeable lack of excitement, with second-hand rolling stock from the mainland but two new tank engines which were painted light blue, and did service for over forty years. Though there were initially only five season-ticket holders on this line and no goods traffic was carried it was ultimately to gain control over half the island network and an ascendancy over all its rivals. In the days of its power and glory it was to be known as the Isle of Wight Central Railway.

For rivals there were and that is what made island railway history so amusing. There was no question here of one big concern scooping the pool. None of the interested parties, I suppose, commanded the necessary finance. In any case, the success of railways in this isolated pocket was somewhat problematical. It was a question of starting a line here, then starting another one there if the first was successful. So three separate companies arose, the I.W. Central, further east the Isle of Wight Railway serving Ryde, Sandown and Ventnor, and, ten years later, a highly individualistic company determined to run

Shanklin, old village
(overleaf) Sandown

its own affairs, the Freshwater, Yarmouth and Newport Railway. Each company painted its engines a different colour, each had a different scale of fares and each did its own advertising. This sometimes led to extravagant statements, such as the I.W. Railway's assertion that Sandown was a convenient place to alight for Newport (which happened to be on the Central Railway) or the Central's claim that Ventnor was an excellent spot from which to reach Freshwater and Alum Bay, and so it was if you happened to want a ten-mile onward trip by horse-drawn coach.

For over fifty years until 1923, when the Southern Railway took over the whole island network, not, be it said, without a protracted fight from the Freshwater and Yarmouth which was the least prosperous of all the lines, fifty-five miles of track were run by the three separate companies. That, it might be thought, was complicated enough, but in fact it represented a simplification of previous conditions. At different times in the last decades of the nineteenth century no less than six companies had operated. After the Cowes and Newport, the railway from Ryde to Ventnor had been next on the map and the opening of its first section to Shanklin was a joyous affair. The station was modest, the train had only three coaches, but the engine with its tall funnel possessed a smart copper dome and a horse-drawn vehicle was waiting to convey the breathless passengers to their lodgings in the town. No one in Shanklin overlooked the importance of this event and two days later the *Isle of Wight Times* broke into verse:

> Hark, hark! I hear a whistle shrill
> And lo! The puffing steam
> All over hedge and through the hill,
> What, am I in a dream!
>
> Strangers at Shanklin may well stare
> With joy and admiration
> When they behold a railway there,
> And also railway station.

A couple of years later, a third company started a line from Ryde to Newport. It remained independent while the line was under

The old Ryde to Cowes train (overleaf)
Hovercraft, Ryde

construction and then merged with the Cowes and Newport. Meanwhile, a fourth party of pioneers was pressing westwards from Sandown to link up in a wide loop with Newport in a separate project known as the Isle of Wight (Newport Junction) Railway. The object of this enterprise is obscure. It was expensive as it entailed building a viaduct over the Medina and despite strenuous efforts by the company to persuade the public that the most convenient and picturesque route from Sandown to Ryde (six miles by the rival I.W. Railway) was to circle round by Newport over fifteen miles of countryside no one seems to have believed it, the company went bankrupt and the line was absorbed by the Cowes and Newport into a network which it now styled the Isle of Wight Central Railway.

But more projects were on the way. The Freshwater, Yarmouth and Newport was planned in 1880 by a fifth company. The directors were ambitious and apparently somewhat irascible. They schemed to link up with a mainland route to Southampton; they quarrelled with their contractors and tried unsuccessfully to impound some of their gear. After an agreement with the Central Railway to use their Newport station and a trial trip with two open trucks jammed with top-hatted gentlemen, the new line was opened in 1888. For some years all went well, although purists noted that the halts advertised as Calbourne and Shalfleet were in fact miles from either village. Then an argument blew up with the Central. Their rate for the use of Newport station was too high, it was claimed, but the Central was adamant, so the F.Y. & N. set up its own Newport station in a corrugated iron shed and forced through-passengers to trudge from one to the other. Now, alas, like all the others, this noble and militant enterprise is no more. Its Freshwater terminus has been demolished and replaced by a neat factory manufacturing springs and lovers now stroll over the bridge below the church and then turn left down the leafy and trackless line to Yarmouth. A sixth and last company, calling itself the Shanklin and Chale Railway, decided on mature reflection that St. Boniface Down and the Undercliff were inimical to trains, switched its ambitions northwards and built the Newport, Godshill and St. Lawrence Railway which was opened in 1897, promptly taken over by the Central line and now lies, buried beneath greenery, as a track for rabbits.

Today, visitors wanting to recapture these glories can go to Havenstreet, south-west of Ryde, and travel one mile eastwards on a genuine antique island train by courtesy of the I.O.W. Steam Locomotive Society. It is to be hoped too that some museum will find room for selected items from the stud of locomotives which were all old-age pensioners when they went out of service, built in the 1890s and much loved by railway enthusiasts for their cast-iron chimneys, brass-work and jaunty little cabs. To a layman such hoary antiquity seems an astonishing fact. I had always imagined that engines wear out fairly quickly, particularly the islanders' which have formidable gradients to climb and with the fuss they made always seemed to be working under protest. All that, apparently, was deceptive. Engines are very tough and there was one, named the Bonchurch, which on arrival was accidentally dropped in St. Helens harbour where it stayed for several days before being fished out to perform good service for forty-five years.

In the palmy days of the railways there was hardly a place of importance which was not visited by these happy little snorters, drawing three or at the most five antique wooden coaches, sometimes interspersed with goods trucks. Most of the coaches were four-wheelers and had already reached an advanced age before ever they left the mainland, the pride of the collection being a magnificent piece of architecture with clerestory windows which trundled about for a total of sixty-two years. There were no corridor trains here, of course, and if the coach had originally been fitted with a lavatory this was converted on arrival into a small compartment—after all, island journeys were short. All the same, the distinction between 1st and 3rd class was jealously preserved, the trains were efficient though slow and there was never a serious accident in the island. Though they always carried a fair amount of freight, the peak was reached with over 200,000 tons in 1901 and fell slowly ever after. The island railways were never strong financially, despite expensive fares. But far from impairing the local beauty, they gave liveliness to the scenery, lilliputian railways in an island where everything is mercifully smaller in scale than on the mainland.

Part of the charm of railway engines consists, of course, in the fact that they are forbidden fruit. I should very much like to drive an engine, but will never be allowed to. Few people have the space or money to set up their own Bluebell railway, and as for middle-aged men fooling about with model trains in their attics, that seems to me slightly potty. No, only the real thing will do, but it is precisely the real thing which is reserved to a band of blue-coated initiates whose childhood dream may never have been engine-driving at all. What a terrible thought. And yet there is great satisfaction to be derived from doing for pleasure what others perform as their business and this, it seems to me, would apply one hundred per cent to driving an engine, just as it applies in other spheres: building a brick wall, for instance, or in olden times sailing a boat.

If this seems obvious today, it was by no means clear to our ancestors. One sees pictures of Elizabethan gentlemen hawking, riding or playing bowls, but never building a wall. Yet bricks were a novelty in their time. Why did they not try their hand? Similarly yachting— from the Dutch *yaghten*, to hunt—was unheard of as a pastime until in 1646 the future Charles II, when staying in the Channel Islands, sailed a small boat round the coasts for pleasure. After the Restoration it is said that the Dutch East India Company presented him with a 20-ton sailing boat which he took much interest in. At about the same time the word "yacht" first came into use, though to begin with it was confined to a kind of official boat used for conveying important persons. Gentlemen, of course, would not do manual work, would never lay their hand on the tiller, and so, whatever the boats were called, the pleasure of steering your own craft remained unknown for many years to come. It was not until 1758 that Fielding, at the start of his voyage to Lisbon when he saw ships sailing down the Thames below Greenwich, came out in print with what seems to have been the first suggestion of pleasure sailing. It would afford, he thought, "the highest degree of amusement to sail ourselves in little vessels of our own, contrived only for our own use and accommodation", though he expected that the sport would be costly. At the time he wrote this, the first pleasure yachting was taking place on the Thames.

But messing about with boats as a general pastime had to wait until the wealthier classes, those that could afford holidays by the sea, took an interest in salt water. And this was an exceedingly slow development. Since the earliest times, no one in England had gone to the coast for pleasure. Then in the seventeenth century voices were raised in favour of sea-water as a universal panacea, to drink, not to bathe in. In the eighteenth, the little dip was also considered healthful and visitors were attracted to Scarborough, Margate and Worthing. George III popularized Weymouth. Later, the Prince Regent took Brighthelmstone in his chubby embrace. But still there was no sailing, except by professional boatmen who fished and, in the Isle of Wight, steered pilot cutters or smuggled. In the island we must not imagine any visitor lingering by the shore until well on into the Napoleonic wars. There was nothing to do there except admire the mighty forces of nature and the odd ship or two and then scuttle thankfully inland. In Ryde, Fielding could barely find enough to eat. As late as 1792, Cowes was not much frequented, either. Its main activity was shipbuilding, which had been going on since Elizabethan times, and now the two shipyards were producing three-deckers and frigates for the navy. There were no facilities for visitors and in the war which followed there was little time for pleasure. The roadstead, one day to become the Mecca of yachtsmen, was filled with merchantmen awaiting convoy from warships, and the townsmen were kept busy provisioning them.

But Boney had not yet been laid by the heels when a trickle of visitors began to arrive, swelling considerably after the Duke of Gloucester came to Cowes in 1811. In that year there was already a theatre and concerts were given at the Fountain Inn (still in existence) where Hampshire papers reported that one Mr. Griesley "particularly distinguished himself upon the hautboy". The fun, indeed, was fast and furious—balls lasting until dawn and an exhibition of "Mr. Clarke's philosophical fireworks from air only", whatever they might be. The male visitors found a nice beach between the Castle and Egypt Point and began to bathe; machines were set up; the shore became the resort of much fashionable company. Then smacks were fitted up as pleasure vessels and some of the wealthier people even bought their own private boats. From these they watched sailing matches between the local fishermen, and in 1813 the Duke of Gloucester patronized the contests which thereafter gained in importance and became known as the Isle of Wight Annual Regatta. Two years later, spurred by the professionals, the amateur gentlemen were running their own race and founding a yacht club, Commodore, the Hon. Charles Pelham, later Lord Yarborough. Qualifications were simple: an entrance fee, good social standing and the possession of a yacht of over a certain tonnage. In 1817, the Prince Regent joined, followed by the royal Princes, and when he became King the title was changed to the Royal Yacht Club. For a long time yet, though, it was not primarily a club for yacht racing, but a social institution whose members occasionally held private races with no rules bar the obvious one that the winner takes all.

They were imbued with a ferocious competitive spirit, these early yachtsmen, and the first cup race in 1826 produced an ugly incident when two boats collided and the enraged crews started a free fight in which sundry gentlemen were temporarily felled with blows on the head. In those years the racing was mainly confined to three large cutters owned by the great enthusiasts Lord Belfast, Mr. Smith and Mr. Weld. After a number of hard-fought contests it was found necessary to tighten up the rules. One of them, which stated that a yacht on the port tack should always give way to one on the starboard, had Lord Belfast's wholehearted support. "In the event," declared the spirited peer, "of any vessel on the larboard tack attempting to cross me when on the starboard tack, if I have it in my power I shall cut her in two . . ." Meanwhile, other members of the club, of whom there were soon over a hundred, were pottering about the Solent and sometimes undertaking long voyages to the Mediterranean, fitting their vessels, because of the continued prevalence of French privateers, with a formidable armament. One ship, for instance, the *Scorpion*, a cutter of 110 tons, carried two brass 4-pounders, two 6-pounders and an armoury of pistols and cutlasses in which the crew were diligently trained.

The club grew rapidly in prestige, but Cowes went its way oblivious of the rank and fashion that now thronged the sea-front. There were Carolina rice-ships to be unloaded and their contents put up in barrels for shipment to Holland and Germany. J. Samuel White and Ratsey (then a shipbuilder, not a sail-maker) were still turning out men-of-war. Henry VIII's neglected forts, called the East Cow and the West Cow because the guns made a mooing noise when they were fired, lowered indifferently over labourer and peer. The population of about 2,000 was glad to have the gentry spending money in the town, but no efforts were made to improve it. Old, rat-ridden warehouses clustered on piles by the shore, there were huge pot-holes in the streets, the parade was inches deep in mud. Worst of all, as the *Hampshire Herald* noted with lofty detachment from the mainland, rowdy young persons of both sexes were allowed to mingle with the quality whom they were not averse to insulting. Stung by this stricture, perhaps, the townsmen presented two cups to be contested by members of the club. A King's Cup had already been given in 1827 and the ensuing celebrations had continued, as the *Herald* reported, "until the Blacksmith of Night struck One on the Anvil of Morn".

George IV, William IV, Queen Victoria and the Prince Consort all patronized the club. To gain them the same privileges as British warships in foreign ports, members were allowed to fly the White Ensign, a concession at first extended to other clubs, but later confined to the Royal Yacht Squadron, as the club now came to be known. The predominance of the big cutters began to decline in the 1830s; boats of all rigs and sizes were admitted to the great races which became better organized and attempts were made to devise suitable means of handicapping.

But not every member of the R.Y.S., or indeed of the other yacht clubs that sprang up round the British coasts in the 1840s, pretended to know or care much about yachting. Of the Earl of Cardigan of Crimean notoriety elected in 1849, the following dialogue is recorded with the professional skipper of his boat:

Skipper: "Will you take the helm, My Lord?"

Cardigan: "Will I take what?"

Skipper: "The helm, My Lord."

Cardigan (affably): "No, thank you. I never take anything between meals."

In defence of the abstemious Earl be it said, however, that the wealthy aristocrat or magnate who barely knows one end of his boat from the other is no stranger to the twentieth century. It is said that the famous Sir Thomas Lipton would never have recognized his *Shamrock* if she had not been painted green, and I have heard of one pre-war tycoon who used his splendid yacht merely for dictating business letters, because it was quieter there. Throughout the history of the R.Y.S. there have been many members who were glad to belong to the club more for the social prestige it conferred than from a real interest in yacht racing and this trend was encouraged by the admission of steamers to the Squadron in 1844—"provided they consume their own smoke", stated a facetious resolution of the Committee —and by the fact that Squadron yachts continued to resemble warships rather than racing craft, with a total armament, enough to blow Cowes from its hillside, of four hundred guns.

But this did not quell the ubiquitous and comforting conviction that yacht racing was the prerogative of Englishmen, that they alone excelled in it and that developments in other countries could be safely ignored. It caused a shock, therefore, followed by mild amusement when rumours reached the R.Y.S. in 1851 that a craft was being built in America to challenge the best of the English fleet. Were there yachts in America? No one had heard of them. But the rumour was true and news came shortly from the recently founded New York Yacht Club that it was sending over a "schooner" in the hope of racing against the pick of the Squadron. What was a schooner? Nobody at Cowes could be sure, though it would seem that the first craft of this type was evolved by a colonist named Robinson at Gloucester, Maine, in 1713, its fore-and-aft rig inspired by the general outline of the Mediterranean lateen sail. As the new ship went off the slips, a by-stander had cried: "Look how she schoons!" And Robinson had replied: "A schooner let her be." All this was unknown to the English. At Cowes, the Earl of Wilton, Commodore of the Squadron, blithely accepted the challenge and invited the Americans to stay at the club-house during their visit. In due course, the *America*, principal owner Commodore John C. Stevens, arrived: a fore-and-aft schooner of 170 tons, remarkable for a very fine, hollow-type bow. Flying through the water, this ship carried off the special cup of £100 offered for the race and, in other contests, met almost every notable vessel on the Squadron list and beat them all. Among the losers there was con-sternation, though no one was more incensed than the watermen of Cowes, who considered it was too bad of the Yankees to "upset their gentlemen" by winning. Thereafter, the *America* greatly influenced the design of English yachts, though as yet the cup has never recrossed the Atlantic.

A great transformation was now at hand. Until the death of the Prince Consort the Squadron had been under royal patronage, but no member of the Royal Family had ·taken a close interest in its affairs. High society tended to look askance at people who donned weird dress and spent the summer in an atmosphere of a perpetual stag-party at dilapidated Cowes playing around with boats. But in 1863 the Prince of Wales became a patron, found Cowes, yachting and the club much to his taste and for nineteen years from 1882 was its Com-modore. If Cowes was good enough for the Prince it was more than adequate for anyone else and soon the cream of English society was descending on the little place for the period of Cowes Week when it became the centre of one of the great social functions of the year. The week fitted in nicely between the end of the London season and the recuperative round of the great European spas which began in the autumn. At West Cowes Castle, where the Squadron now had its club-house, eminent males monopolized the building and the seaward platform, wearing short blue jackets whenever the design of their posteriors allowed them to do so. Tucked away on the lawn behind the building, the ladies sat on rickety wicker chairs, gossiping and nibbling at ices. The lawn was their pen, they were not permitted to leave it, and what with hopes that the Prince with his white cap, big cigar and black ebony stick might arrive at any moment and the harrowing knowledge that toilet facilities for the fair sex were non-existent at the castle, the atmosphere was often fraught with conflicting emotions.

The season at Cowes was certainly an ordeal. For at least a whole week the wealthy and famous slept in narrow yacht cabins in the roads or counted themselves lucky to find an expensive attic-bedroom on land. One large family they might be, as it was said, of the nicest and prettiest people in England, but Cowes made few concessions. In fifty years not much had altered apart from an improved steamboat service, the railway to Newport and the telegraph. Otherwise the town, cramped between the sea and a large private estate, was its old incredible self, "a heap of superior dog-kennels", said one writer, "which have been rolled down the hill and brought up full on the edge of the water". Shop-keepers, despite august patronage, were slow to adapt themselves to specialized needs. The chemist sold cigars, the green-grocer chickens, and the ironmonger baited a display of useful hooks in front of his shop with herrings and bleeding pigs' heads.

Amid these informal, not to say eccentric surroundings, the castle preserved the strictest decorum. The Squadron had always been very exclusive and the system of election was so rigid that even the Prince of Wales could not get it changed. The system was simple: whenever there was the slightest doubt about their suitability, applicants for membership were blackballed. And to those who objected, the answer was equally uncompromising: this had always been so, ever since the days when a committee member had openly declared that he was against accepting a man on principle if he did not know him personally. One notorious blackballer on the committee was known as "the piller of society". Rejected applicants were liable to feel very sore at their treatment and the story is told of one individual known as the Pirate who owned a 150-ton schooner with eight brass guns. On being rejected for membership in the 1860s he threatened to blow Cowes

Castle sky-high unless the committee apologized to him, and such was his reputation that the apology was made. Another eager applicant fatally overplayed his hand by greeting a handsome committee member in the street with: "How pleasant it is to see an old Cowes face!"

Those lucky people who did manage to get elected found life at the castle hedged with sacrosanct customs. In the morning-room members wiped their pens at the writing-table in a bowl of shot, as their grandfathers had done. They dined alone at separate tables. They drank "Montagus", consisting of gin, soda and a slice of lemon, because the long-dead Admiral Victor Montagu had invented the drink. To consult the weather, hallowed tradition made it necessary to perform a pilgrimage to the platform where the coconut matting was said to crinkle when a damp south-wester was approaching. All this continued up to the First World War and no one did more to maintain the rigid rules than William, the club waiter, a shabby, tobacco-chewing old man who was the biggest snob of all. If sponsored, certain non-members of the Squadron were allowed to walk on the seaward platform. Access to the castle itself was jealously guarded by one Myers, a naval signalman. With Sir Richard Collinson, K.C.B. William had the following encounter:

Sir Richard: "I'm Deputy-Master of Trinity House."

William: "Then you can walk about here and as far as Mr. Myers' box."

Sir Richard: "But I want some luncheon."

William: "Then you can't have any."

Sir Richard: "But I thought we had the entrée?"

William: "You won't get no entrées 'ere!"

Experts now consider that the best period in yacht racing at Cowes was between 1890 and 1900, when amateurs started to steer their own craft instead of professional helmsmen. I feel, though, that this judgement is somewhat academic and few of those yachtsmen who now sail their boats round the Wight in summer would probably care whether their efforts lie in a good, bad or indifferent period. Nor is there much point, I suppose, in drawing comparisons between the glamour of Cowes in Edward VII's time and today. Cowes Week still offers plenty of glamour, though Kaiser William is no longer there, competing in his *Meteor* against his uncle's *Britannia*, both ships sailed by an English skipper with an English crew, both designed by the same Scottish designer. The Kaiser left a trail of outrageous stories behind him, how he had stamped and fumed when he lost a race and blown down the ear-trumpet of a deaf English Admiral, but as Kaiser he belongs to the world of pre-1914 and so to another life. But we do read with a certain nostalgia of the year 1909 when four reigning monarchs attended Cowes Week, King Edward in the *Victoria and Albert*, Tsar Nicolas in the *Standart*, Kaiser William in the *Hohenzollern*, and the King of Spain with his racing yacht *Hispania*. "Ashore and afloat", we are told, "there were dinner parties and balls. Steam launches, with gleaming brass funnels and slender cutters and gigs, pulled by their crews at the long white oars, plied between the yachts and the Squadron steps. By day, the sails of the racing yachts spread across the blue waters of the Solent like the wings of giant butterflies, by night riding lights and lanterns gleamed and shone like glow-worms against the onyx waters and fireworks burst and spent themselves in the night sky. And over this splendid scene presided the King, a genial, portly, yet always majestic figure."

In 1893, the Prince of Wales had ordered *Britannia* from the famous designer, G. L. Watson, in order to compete on equal terms with the Kaiser who the year before had bought an English yacht named *Thistle* and rechristened her *Meteor*. Because of her broad round hull *Britannia* was known as a "skimming dish" and was a first-class racing cutter, a great advance on existing designs which tended to produce the "plank-on-edge", a narrow boat with an immense lead keel which ploughed through the water and despite a huge sail area was slow. Each year the competition between the King and his nephew was renewed. There were four versions of *Meteor*, but only the last was built in Germany and sailed by an all-German crew and only the second succeeded in beating *Britannia*.

Meanwhile, another colourful figure had appeared on the racing scene, Sir Thomas Lipton, the millionaire-errand boy, teetotaller, non-smoker, non-gambler, who lived only for his business of selling tea and over a period of thirty years was five times unsuccessful challenger for the America's Cup. The only reason why he challenged at all was because he thought it would help to sell his beverage—and how right he was! After the first failures he began to realize that losing could be just as useful for this purpose as winning and he set himself out, as well he might, knowing barely one end of a boat from another, to succumb with charm and good humour, to such effect that the

Americans eventually presented him with a gold loving cup inscribed "To the World's Best Loser". Lipton's five *Shamrocks* and his steam yacht *Erin* were for years familiar sights at Cowes, but he was only elected to the Squadron in the last year of his life when he was nearly eighty and by then the compliment was obviously double-edged. So, when he heard the news, the old man merely raised an eyebrow and blandly inquired in his thick Scottish accent: "Tell me, where are the offices of yon club that I've joined?"

But by then, in the 1930s, the attitude of the election committee was slowly changing. The wealthy aristocrats of Edwardian days had left considerably less affluent heirs and a new era had dawned when the men who owned big racing yachts were all business magnates and for better or worse some of them had to be elected to the Squadron. This was known as the period of the Beerage and the Peerage. Besides Sopwith, whose *Endeavour I* nearly won back the America's Cup from Mike Vanderbilt's *Rainbow* in 1934, Lord Camrose, Ernest Guinness, Richard Hennessy and John Gretton of "Bass" were all members of the Squadron. They possessed huge cutters known as racing machines, because their owners did not live aboard them and their cabins were fitted with the minimum of comfort.

Meanwhile, under George V as Admiral of the Squadron, the males were still bitterly defending their entrenched position at the castle. It was not until the 1930s that ladies were allowed to lunch and dine within the precincts, and then only on certain days and within certain hours. Before that, they had only been allowed inside the club to view the cups and to set foot on the sacred platform on the last day of the regatta to watch the fireworks. Otherwise, the back lawn had still been their territory where gossip amid a welter of ice-cream and strawberries had contrasted with hearty nautical talk laced with gin on the seaward side of the castle. There was no ladies' room until the 1920s and women in trousers were banished to outer darkness until 1938, when they were allowed to appear in them out of doors, except during Cowes Week, which was the time when many most wanted to wear them.

The 1930s were considered the boom years for Cowes yachting. Americans flooded the town for the British-American Cup sailed by teams of little 6-metre boats, and the ocean race from Cowes round the Fastnet Rock to Plymouth. The anchorage was dominated by the huge cutters *Shamrock V*, *Endeavour* and the chairman of Woolworth's

Velsheda. Today the yachts are smaller in size, but the popularity of the Cowes season, which lasts from May to September, is greater than ever. In some races, as many as one thousand five hundred people are competing at the same moment. The Round-the-Island race in June produces a spectacular start of over three hundred boats. Practically all the classes of boat to be seen round the English coasts in summer find their way to Cowes: 14-foot dinghies, Dragons, Flying Fifteens, Redwings, Swallows, South Coast One-Designs, X-Boats and Solent Sunbeams. As for the Squadron, its present-day annals remain to be written, but meanwhile it may well be that blotting-paper is now supplied in the morning-room and it is not entirely unheard of for two members to dine together. The island is proud of the Yacht Squadron, but prouder still of Cowes, the premier yachting port in the British Isles facing the best yachting waters in the world. The guide book is fittingly boastful of this, but down by the esplanade some of those wooden warehouses can still be seen and, secure in the knowledge that Cowes Week has come to stay, the inhabitants are content with their town just as it is: an expanded village, modest, unpretentious and in parts picturesque.

X

VICTORIA AT OSBORNE

In the 1860s a German visitor to the island, nosing with thoroughness into its beauties, took the public coach from Ventnor to Blackgang. The journey, "with fiery steeds in rapid flight", took over an hour, up-hill, down-dale through scenery which to the stranger resembled paradise. St. Catherine's lighthouse was just coming into view when the coach turned north and drove through rising parkland towards the Sandrock Hotel, a famous inn which Queen Victoria had visited with her mother over thirty years before. "An incomparable position," noted the tourist—a sloping lawn facing the sea amidst wooded hills with gay flower-beds and a comfortable, countrified little building surrounded by a veranda where ivy mingling with roses climbed up the pillars and over the roof. "Ideal for a honeymoon!" declared a young Scottish lady, descending with her Mama from the coach, preparatory, no doubt, to resting in the hotel before visiting, as perhaps the Princess Victoria had done, the no less famous medicinal spring of Doctor Waterworth.

Many years before, the doctor, when scrambling about the shore, had come across a gush of turbid water cascading down the rocks. He had analysed it and quickly come to the conclusion that here were the makings of a profitable enterprise. The water was fizzing with carbonic acid gas and contained in solution potent household remedies, unfailing in their volcanic effect on the human system, in the form of Epsom and Glauber salts. Moreover, and this was a useful attribute considering that people are never averse to achieving health through suffering, the water was nauseating to the taste. So the doctor built an elaborate shrine over the source of the spring with a gothic stone arch, trefoil window and an inscription in Latin, in which language crudities for some reason sound more acceptable, which meant: "The water which flows here is good for those weak in the head and the belly." He then advertised his spring as "aluminous and intensely chalybeate" and invited the public to perform the by no means easy ascent to the shrine where for a modest sum they could partake of the health-giving fluid. The doctor made a lot of money and no doubt many digestions were ruined, but the stimulating pagan-Christian atmosphere insured success and for many years hypochondriacal Victorians laboured up the precipitous path, as a form of penance or in search of health, they hardly knew which.

I am not suggesting that the spring made much impression on the Princess Victoria, but the charming hotel, the wild scenery, the wooded slopes by East Cowes which she saw on the same visit when laying the foundation stone of a church left pleasant memories of the island in her youthful mind, and these slumbered in her thoughts until five years after her marriage when circumstances revived them with startling brightness. These, it need hardly be said, centred on Albert, the adorable young man with the beautiful profile, the lovely mouth, the delicate moustachioes and the *very* slight whiskers to whom she had proposed, as was fitting for a Queen, and married, her heart dissolving almost with love, in 1840. Since then, four children had been born and the early relationship between their parents had turned from one of dominance by the Queen into an idyllic partnership where each ruled in complementary spheres, Albert intellectually and Victoria emotionally. Tired of the barrack atmosphere of Buckingham Palace set amidst the gaping Londoners and of the massive medievalism of Windsor, for herself she now longed for a country retreat, and for Albert, scope for his undoubted talents, pitifully thwarted in existing palaces, as landscape gardener, architect, interior decorator. Such a retreat, if it could be found, she pictured as love-nest and family home, designed entirely by the beloved hands, a mirror of his personality where every corridor, every glade would be an extension of himself and she could live in a giant projection of the man she adored. This dream, she discovered, could be fulfilled at Osborne.

They went over together to East Cowes, noted the sloping parks, the private beach, the glimpse of the Solent and Spithead with its warships (so interesting to Albert), the possibility of complete seclusion and bought the estate of two thousand acres immediately: their property, not the Crown's, as it was paid for out of the Queen's private purse.

Albert then got to work, "free", as the Queen joyfully noted, "from all Woods and Forests and other charming Departments, who really are the plague of one's life." First, the house. An existing structure was knocked down and then, because the glimpse of the sea reminded him of Naples, he made rough plans—details to be worked out by a competent builder—of something quite new in England, a Palladian mansion in the Italian manner with flag-tower, bell-tower, court-yard, balconies and a corridor running right round the building, partly open to the air at first-floor level in the style of an Italian loggia. The grey surfaces were severe, the angles were sharp, relieved only by one deep bay in the royal apartments, and the big oblong windows, the portals, the colonnades gaped coldly on the gentle English countryside like holes tunnelled for gasping occupants in a tropic clime. When built, Osborne glowered like a factory or a penitentiary over the surrounding fields, arrogant and alien. But Albert had designed it and Victoria was overjoyed.

The park and gardens were, indeed, enchanting and these, too, had been planned by Albert. At the back of the house, which faced towards the Solent, a formal garden on two levels was made, with fountains, stone balustrades, circular flower-beds and a pergola. This was a pleasant transition between the severity of the building and the natural appearance of the park which sloped with well-clipped grass towards the Solent. Here Albert took care to create a thoroughly English atmosphere, planting clumps of oaks and elms, many of them with his own hands, contriving rides and vistas to give glimpses of the nearby sea and dotting the slopes with gazebos. Nearer the house, in keeping with its exotic appearance, ilexes, cork trees, cedars, deodars and Mediterranean pines were packed, partly for the sake of privacy.

To this home, with only the private apartments in the Pavilion Wing as yet finished, the Queen and her husband arrived to spend their first night in September 1846. Albert had been busy on the interior, too. In the corridors, garter-blue alcoves topped with gilded plaster shells provided niches for family busts. Between them were plaster reliefs in imitation of famous classical friezes. The floors were covered with encaustic tiles intricately laid to reproduce the designs on Turkey carpets. Marble statues, huge pedestal vases of hollow glass, heavy chandeliers for the private drawing-room, Landseers, portraits of the Queen's dogs, furniture made of the antlers of deer shot in the royal parks, vivid carpets with crimson, orange and turquoise flowers, the Albert Marbles including a statue of the Prince in Roman armour, statuettes of ponies and Highland ghillies, massive mahogany furniture,

*Boatbuilding on
the island*

choice porcelain under glass domes, marble-topped china cupboards with ormolu decorations, marble replicas of the limbs of the royal children resting on velvet cushions—slowly, through the succeeding months and years, these choice items were shifted into place to give the interior a thoroughly cosy appearance.

Meanwhile, on this, one of the happiest days of their lives, Victoria, eagerly clinging to the arm of her husband, had sailed over in her little two-funnelled steamboat to take possession of her new home. The royal couple and their suite were in high spirits. The doors were flung open and everything looked so wonderfully new and fresh; there was no smell of paint and no suggestion of damp. For good luck one of the Maids of Honour threw an old shoe after the Queen as she crossed the threshold and that night at dinner all were conscious that this was the beginning of a momentous new chapter in the royal lives. The Queen's eyes were shining, but the Prince was solemn and after dinner, quite naturally but with much feeling, he said: "We have a hymn in Germany for such occasions. It begins . . ." And then he quoted Luther, lines which asked God to "bless our going out and our coming in". Soon after this, they retired. For a while the lamps burned brightly in the first-floor sitting-room and could have been seen far out over the Solent. Then they were turned down and on this night we can imagine the Queen and her husband coming for the first time through the French windows and on to the little semicircular balcony beneath its striped awning to gaze at the moonlit park, as they did so often in later years.

A captivating scene. Down towards the sea, gleaming like a promise of eternity in the distance, slopes the silvered park. Dark grey trees loom against paler grass. The straight drive, almost white now under the moon, slants down towards a slight dip in a dark recess by the shore. After the formalities of London, the fret, the smoke, here is silent nature, seclusion, at last a place of one's own. The press may bicker and ministers will still have to be seen, but from now on there will always be Osborne and this enchanted park. Victoria loves it for Albert's sake. The clusters of young trees, the white ribbon of drive, those little shrubs beside it that one day will grow into smooth balls of clipped yew, all have been planned by him: they are a glimpse into his soul. Albert loves it with a German's longing to find God in nature, and because it reminds him of his childhood home in Rosenau and because he created this scene.

Cowes Week

And now, from the older trees, shrouded in pale blue mist, comes a clear, echoing trill and then a crescendo of single notes.

"Hörst du? Der Nachtigall! . . ."

They listen with bated breath. Tears of ecstasy are in her eyes. She clings yet tighter to his arm. Then the little woman, still in her crinoline, eases her way through the French windows, carefully past the mass of furniture already installed, pauses to gaze fondly at the twin writing-tables already placed side by side, with the blotters not eighteen inches apart, where tomorrow they will work together at the stacks of documents, and so to bed in the new house, where on the floor above the children are long since asleep, to dream of a long white road leading into the future with only two figures upon it, walking confidently forward, arm in arm.

The idyll lasted for fifteen years. The house was enlarged to provide apartments for visiting royalty and accommodation for the household. The Prince, with the solemn conscientiousness that characterized him in all things, developed the estate, started a model farm which actually made money, and half a mile from the house installed a chalet for the children which came in sections from Switzerland. Here the youngsters, Victoria, Edward, Alice, Alfred, Helena, Louise, Arthur, Leopold and Beatrice, in turn studied the art of domestic economy, gardening, cooking, carpentering. There was a fully fitted kitchen, a larder, a pantry and a dining-room where they sometimes entertained their parents to tea with buns and pastry which they had made themselves. The boys grew vegetables and dug in the garden. The girls busied about, acting the proud housewife, washing, ironing, cooking, pickling and no doubt making a terrible mess. But their days were filled with joy. The chalet was their own, mercifully shielded from the pomp of the big mansion, and there were fields and woods all around where they could pick posies for their Mama, climb the trees, shout and roll in the grass. How often, in later years, scattered over the face of Europe in Berlin, Hesse or Schleswig-Holstein, mewed in huge palaces, caught in the web of high politics, must they have looked back with longing to those summer days which never seemed to end when with the marvellous concentration of childhood their youthful minds were absorbed in baking a jam tart, or picking a bunch of marigolds or making a box to be sawn and nailed from pale planks of sweet-smelling wood. Today we can go over this chalet, by far the prettiest building in the whole estate, visit the kitchen imagining childish arms up to the elbows in flour and in a thatched outhouse see the gardening tools and the wheel-barrows, each with its owner's initials: "P.W.", "P.L.", "Pss. A.".

Twice a year the family came to Osborne, from the end of December to the end of January and from mid-July to the end of August. The Queen bathed from an elegant machine with a porch and removable steps. Albert was always up, winter and summer, bv seven o'clock preparing the day's paper work in the sitting-room. The children romped. Strange frock-coated men with heavy briefcases came over the Solent for audiences and consultations. Except to go to church at Whippingham there was seldom need to leave the grounds and the islanders did not see much of their royal neighbours. But they were proud of their presence and sightseers flooded to Osborne to stand outside the gates, sensing if not seeing the Queen.

Then came the great calamity. At Windsor, on the night of 14th December, 1861, the Prince Consort died of typhoid and the Queen plunged into a bottomless pit of grief and despair. Once already, when her mother had died in the previous February, her horrified family had seen the floodgate of distress suddenly flung wide open. There had been rivers of tears, unending paroxysms of grief, and this for a woman from whom she had been estranged for years. Was it remorse? Albert had humoured her, tried to dispel rumours that she was going insane. But only in her own time, very slowly, with many backward glances had she rallied and resumed her functions, leaving many people with the strong impression that there was an unaccountable disparity between the strength of her despair and its apparent cause. But with the loss of the Beloved there was cause indeed for self-abandon. On the day after she had heard him murmur his dying "Gutes Frauchen", she was hurried on the advice of King Leopold to Osborne, stunned, not crying, like a lifeless puppet. Confined to her rooms where the tears at last started to flow, she would admit only two people to her presence, Princess Alice and her Woman of the Bedchamber, Lady Augusta Bruce. Her wails could be heard even in the corridors. State papers she signed with utter indifference as though they were blank sheets. Warned that a Privy Council must be held, she said she was no longer concerned with earthly things. But the Council took place while the Queen sat in an adjoining room with the curtains drawn and the door ajar. For the Household, moving about like shadows in the cluttered mansion that now felt like a tomb, it was a terrible time.

Lady Bruce wrote to her sister that life seemed suddenly extinguished. Someone who came down on business from Windsor noticed that everyone had become thinner and there were lines of care on every face. As the weeks passed, the Queen's grief seemed to increase rather than diminish. She was totally heartbroken.

With rebellious self-torture, the Queen ordered the Prince's belongings to be left exactly where they had been when he had last used them, even down to the carelessly abandoned pocket-handkerchief. From that time, a photograph of his corpse was hung a foot above the unoccupied pillow in every bed in which she slept. Hot water and a clean nightshirt were laid out for him every evening. When we visit Osborne and see his sticks and umbrellas still in their stand by his dressing-room we are reminded of this terrible time in the Queen's life and we seem to hear that sweet voice of hers that Ellen Terry likened to a silver stream flowing over golden stones speaking with infinite weight and sorrow: "I lived only through him, the Heavenly Angel . . . My only wish is to join him soon . . . I try to comfort myself by knowing that he is always near me, although invisible . . ."

But the turning-point came at last when after her long sojourn with the dead she returned to life, though a changed woman with other, as yet little seen characteristics predominant, and always in black. This, too, we can visualize. Fourteen months after Albert's death she still weeps very much, but she is occasionally seen now about the house and garden. She meets her ministers, she agitates the Household with admonitory notes despatched from her first-floor sanctum. A new personality appears: tyrannical, petulant, self-indulgent to the point of inertia. As yet, since that dreadful night, she has never once smiled. But then, on a morning in March, after breakfast which she always takes alone, she glances through a window, and there, coming up that long white drive towards the terrace, is John Brown, "good Brown", the handsome, red-haired ghillie whom Albert chose for her at Balmoral over eleven years ago. With him is her highland pony and the little pony-cart that she used to drive herself. A flood of memory returns. In this brawny figure, whose confident walk and forthright speech she so well remembers, is comfort and security at last. Her heart tells her this almost despite herself. So, half an hour later, Victoria is seated in the pony-cart and Brown is leading her off towards the park, while Lady Augusta watches in mild astonishment from the terrace, for she has been told that it will be unnecessary for her to accompany them. From time to time Brown turns and says something to the Queen and, miracle of miracles, Victoria is actually smiling.

She was to reign for another thirty-nine years, through national anxieties and renewed private sorrows, intensely unpopular for a long period as the royal recluse unseen by her people, but slowly mounting to an apotheosis as the all-wise, all-benevolent mother of the greatest empire in world history. Her life at Osborne was never recorded by herself and contemporary writers who tried to penetrate the veil of her privacy were lucky if they got as far as the ground-floor rooms escorted by the Scottish housekeeper. But here and there, from members of the Household, we gain glimpses of a life in the big mansion which sorely tried them all. At the centre of the hive sat the Queen Bee, wrapped in her mourning, bunched in a voluminous gown long out of fashion from which the crinoline had been removed. The presence of the Beloved Dead was felt everywhere. Doors swung silently to and fro, the servants glided over thickly carpeted floors, everyone spoke in muted tones. The Queen had to be humoured, her demands, however extraordinary, complied with at once. Nobody dared to argue. But then few people were admitted to her presence. With the Private Secretary business was transacted by means of notes which flew up and down stairs twice daily. The forthright, quick-tempered but devoted John Brown, soon raised to the status of permanent indoor personal servant and then given the title of Esquire and a house near Balmoral, was the only attendant in permanent favour. He had access to the Queen at all times, could bully her in his thick Scottish accent, arrange her clothing for her, advise, admonish, possess her almost—and she undoubtedly enjoyed it. In summer we see Brown hovering solicitously while the Queen has her breakfast in a tent on the lawn, remotely accompanied by bagpipes. We see him glowering in the orange shade of a big marquee, her summer work-room, where, with an expression as though she were swallowing poison, she interviews Mr. Gladstone. Gladstone, in later years, is sitting close to her at dinner, exasperating her with a long tirade on Irish Home Rule until Brown, standing behind her chair, interrupts him with a tap on the shoulder and a harsh: "You've said enuf!" He calls Victoria "Wumman", shouts "Hey!" after her, and when he feels like it contradicts her flatly. By everyone except herself he is cordially detested. Some say that his ever-ready tears which the Queen ascribes to a soft heart are due to hard liquor. It is rumoured that he smokes in his bedroom, that his hold over the Queen is due to some link with Albert; perhaps he acts as a psychic medium. But the secret of his power seems more obvious than that. To the lonely widow in the gaunt mansion he offers the chance to lay aside the Queen at times and become an ordinary person. With everyone else, including her own children when they are grown up, this is impossible.

So Brown, bursting into her cocoon with his earthy wit and gritty personality, has wooed her from her melancholia. By slow adaptation she has slowly realized that there is a satisfying role for her to play in the world of reality, the role of universal mother. From Osborne where the affairs of all, from chambermaid to equerry, are her personal concern, her mind goes out with maternal affection to her far-flung family, her people, her Empire. At point-blank range, admittedly, she seems managerial rather than motherly. Females are reprimanded for wearing rouge. Mixed ice-hockey on the Barton pond will *not* take place, its crude rough-and-tumble might embarrass the ladies. Nobody must touch the statues on the ground floor, the fact that they revolve on their bases does *not* mean that they are playthings. The Princesses may picnic with non-royal persons as attendants, but *not* as companions; Papa would *not* have approved. None of these rules is given verbally; they descend in a snowstorm of notes from the higher regions.

Periodically, the Queen in her carriage with outriders tours the estate or goes driving in the island to Cowes, Newport or Ryde. This is the signal for members of the Household to escape to the park where they find it prudent to scatter like ants and walk singly, along different paths, until she returns. There are many acts of kindness to local people, but they can be thankful, all the same, that they do not live under the royal eye. Like a diminutive general she marches un-announced into a cottage on the estate. "May I inspect?" "Delighted, Ma'am . . ." Then she sails upstairs, pokes about, sniffs the atmosphere, runs a gloved hand over ledges and descends, if the occupants are lucky, all smiles. "I am very pleased. It is all very clean. Very clean. *Beautiful!*" Stories of these raids and her wider excursions soon spread about the island. There was the girl who was tricycling along the New-port road when the royal carriage drew up and stopped. "What is that object?" came in clear, silvery tones from the back. "A tricycle,

Your Majesty." "Really. Most interesting. May I see?" The Queen was fascinated and, soon after, the girl was summoned to Osborne to demonstrate. Victoria, if the story can be believed, took one or two turns round the terrace herself, though she ultimately decided with reluctance that tricycling had certain drawbacks as a royal pastime. Then there was the story, charming as he told it, of the estate worker at Barton farm. His son, who worked later than himself, had just sat down to a solitary midday dinner when the Queen came in with two of the Princesses. The boy fled in fright. The ladies sat down at the table and the Queen sampled the dinner. " 'Ah!' she says, munching a potato. 'They's better than wot we gets up at Osborne!' "

On through the seventies and eighties the Queen returns twice yearly to Osborne. Long ago, it seems, her eldest son married the beautiful Princess Alexandra of Denmark. They came to Osborne for their honeymoon and the people of Cowes draped their houses with greenery and hung out a banner: "Welcome, Danish rose!" Long ago, too, Victoria the Princess Royal sailed away to marry Frederick, the Crown Prince of Prussia. Now they have a son William with a withered arm, and the Queen's unerring insight already tells her that one day he will become an international problem. Then in Whippingham church another daughter was married, Helena to Prince Christian of Schleswig-Holstein. Before long, Beatrice, the youngest, will find a husband in Prince Henry of Battenberg. Unable to dispense with "baby" Beatrice, her companion and comfort for so many years, the Queen will persuade them to live with her, Prince Henry as Governor of the island.

But that happy arrangement is yet to come. At the moment she is picking primroses in the Osborne woods for Mr. Disraeli, that fascinating man who calls her his "fairy" and has made her Empress of India. In due course there will be a Durbar Room at Osborne, designed by the father of Rudyard Kipling, Curator of the Lahore Central Museum: sixty feet of heavily carved teak, surmounted by plastered walls and ceiling loaded with ornamentation, a plaster peacock above the chimneypiece and small oriels containing seated figures of the Buddha. This evening, after working at her despatch boxes, writing letters to her numerous progeny abroad and declining once again to open Parliament in person, she will gobble her dinner as she always does, leaving the starved Household to gaze forlornly at the footmen removing their half-finished plates, and then supervise a rehearsal of private theatricals. Yes, the theatre was always her passion, Albert did not disapprove and so now, seated centrally in the drawing-room, her face full of animation which her photographs never show, she will put her hand-picked cast through their paces in a little play she has largely rewritten herself, carefully adjusting the parts so that the actors and actresses of royal blood will have a slight *edge* on the others. Meanwhile, she knows that the ladies excluded from the play are planning a *tableau vivant*, a three-tier cake, monstrous in cardboard, with draped figures on the different levels reclining in devotion or aspiring with upheld doves towards a bust of herself on the top. Most gratifying; a truly charming thought. . . .

Before the Franco-Prussian war the Emperor Napoleon with his beautiful Eugénie visited Osborne. In later years came most of the reigning monarchs, the King of Italy, the King of Portugal, the Tsar and Kaiser William. What a trial! Willy particularly, who at one moment wanted to be treated as a fellow-ruler and the next as her devoted grandchild, required the most careful handling. And his noisy jokes at breakfast upset her digestion. There were problems, too, with Bertie, whose indolence, indiscretions and wild life filled her with forebodings. Problems of State. Problems over one Abdul, an Indian servant whom after the death of John Brown she had raised to the rank of her personal teacher of Hindustani. For some reason, the Government objected when she made him her unofficial adviser on Indian affairs. But she was stubborn and before allowing him to drop into oblivion she gave him a bungalow in the Osborne grounds where, to the fury of the Household but with her tacit consent, he resided with a bevy of dusky beauties whom he euphemistically called his "aunts".

There was, above all, the problem of growing old: failing eyesight, aching limbs, a decline in energy on which there were so many demands. But despite personal griefs—she had lost three of her children—and despite a clouding international scene, disasters in South Africa, mounting trouble in Ireland, the Queen's mind and will grew stronger as her body became more feeble. She gave no thought to herself in these last years of her life. When news came of heavy reverses in the Boer War her courage was paramount and she cabled inspiring messages to the troops. Family affairs she settled with customary resolution. When Marie-Louise, the daughter of Princess Helena, was threatened with ostracism by her father-in-law the Duke of Anhalt, the old Queen telegraphed simply: "Tell my granddaughter to come home to me." She travelled to Netley hospital in her wheeled chair and, standing since they were too badly wounded to rise, pinned Victoria Crosses on the chests of her soldiers. In the last year of her life she went to Ireland because Irish regiments had fought gallantly in South Africa and received, despite widespread fears of disorder, a tumultuous welcome. The Silver Jubilee, the Diamond Jubilee had been unforgettable experiences for herself and her people: "Our hearts thy throne." At Osborne, where the rooms He had used stayed frozen to the last pin as he had left them, where old people served and waited on an ailing Queen and in the winter months of 1900 icy draughts blew through the corridors, all were sustained by the knowledge that behind the cold façade, amid the onward creep of death burned glory ineffaceable.

What was it that had given the Queen this heroic vigour towards the close of her life? The proven love of her subjects, patriotism, pride in her long and glorious reign, or the knowledge that an end was coming to her loneliness, that there was not long to wait and that beyond the mists which confronted her, that barrier she would cross in her own bedroom at Osborne, gleamed something that would wipe away all tears? In her book on the Queen, Edith Sitwell imagines the old lady, a week before she died, driving in the gathering dusk towards Osborne. Among the trees by the drive, half dreaming she sees a boy and a girl walking hand in hand. She hears his voice and recognizes it as one she had known many years ago. She thinks she would recognize the face if he turned and looked at her. Then he does turn—and she feels that she is at Windsor again, on the day that she and Albert had joined their lives together.

XI

SOME ISLAND PROBLEMS

THE modern island is coloured by all these scenes from the past: the aged Queen, her eyes clouded with cataract, gazing at the blurred candle-flames at Osborne and saying pathetically: "Everything seems very *dark* suddenly—I *don't* know *why* . . ."; Tennyson in old age holding out his hands to his son to know if they were clean enough for the dinner-table; Sir John Oglander riding up on his middling black horse to play bowls on St. George's Down; and the island labourers in their white smocks, crowning the last load of corn with flowers before sitting down to the harvest supper, with mutton pies, plum puddings and jugs of extra-strong beer—"Home Harvest Stingo". Then pipes of tobacco, grog dispensed from the head of the table where sits "mayster", the farmer, and songs in heroic or sweetly sentimental vein:

> *Her stockings white, her shoes were bright,*
> *The buckles shined like silver,*
> *She had a black and a rollin' eye*
> *And her hair hung down her shoulders.*

> *How old be you, my pretty maid,*
> *How old be you, my honey?*
> *She answered me right cheerfully,*
> *"I'm zebenteen come Zunday . . ."*

Dimly from the past, too, comes talk in village streets in the local dialect, akin to that of Hampshire and Dorset, itself derived from the speech of the Old English race. "I don't want no aaterclaps from ye!" yells one yokel to another, meaning no back answers, on the analogy of thunder. "Hollo, missus! How be ye?" calls another to a woman on her doorstep. "Terrible sluttish today, edden't it?" And this is not an insult, but a reference to the weather. "She did clapperclaa me proper!" confides a married man to a friend, touching a bruise on his cheek planted there by his spouse. "She gid me such a whistersniff in the chops! Mortal titchy she seems today . . ." Indoors, an old man is holding a newspaper upside down because he is illiterate. Not even the picture of a horse with its legs in the air shows him his error; he thinks it has rolled over in the field. Further on, another old man has joined an island Nonconformist sect called the Bryanites and is reading the Bible for the first time in his life. He has been told that it is the literal truth and reads happily until he comes to Genesis 45. There it states: "Joseph my son is yet alive; I will go and see him before I die." Now this, in the old man's opinion, cannot be true, for "yet" in the island dialect means "eaten".

From these leisurely scenes it is an abrupt transition to the island today, flooded each year by a million and a half visitors (250,000 of them day trippers) bringing with them 15,000 vehicles, which swell the island total in the peak holiday week to 56,000, and spending at the very least thirty million pounds. Yet the flood is absorbed by caravan parks, holiday camps and hundreds of hotels and guest houses and the setting of island life is the same as it has always been: the wind-swept downs, the wooded valleys, the ever-moving, ever-mysterious sea. Of the 110,000 inhabitants, two-thirds live in the towns, leaving over two acres per person in the rest of the island. Three-quarters of the whole area is farmland. And not only is the County Council fully alive to the necessity of preserving the scenic beauty, you can confirm that this is being achieved and tourist facilities have not spoilt the island by visiting it in the off-season. You will see at once that there are still large areas of untouched countryside. The holiday camps merge into their cliff-top sites, the caravans disappear for the winter, the rush and bustle subside.

One must remember, too, that in recent years development has only lightly touched the inland villages, except for certain areas where population has increased: the western peninsula, south of Wootton and inland from Seaview at Nettlestone. Elsewhere the population inland has remained largely static and there has been infilling in the villages but little planned expansion. Among a total of thirty-seven villages, shopping facilities are concentrated in nine, of which seven are near the coast. Of the remainder, two have no shops at all and eighteen have only one foodshop. Twelve villages have no public house; in seventeen of them there is no garage or filling-station. There is one cinema in the whole of the Rural District.

I do not quote these figures as evidence of deplorable backwardness, not at all. They show merely that, apart from Newport, the central core of the island has changed very little over the years compared with similar areas so near to holiday coasts on the mainland. As for the coasts themselves, there are longer stretches here of unspoilt cliff and sand than anywhere else in South-East England. Not all of the sixty miles are suitable, of course, for holiday-makers, but at least half the perimeter of the island is idyllic and overcrowding on the Isle of Wight beaches, even at the height of the season, is a myth which no one need fear.

But if the island beauties are to be preserved, there are problems which need to be carefully watched. Since the last war the tourist trade has been steadily expanding, large numbers of the population depend on it for their livelihood, and as the season is short, from May to September, there is naturally strong pressure to go on increasing the facilities for holiday-makers so as to expand the trade to the maximum. Without careful control this might lead some day to the destruction of the very beauties which visitors come to enjoy, despite the fact that areas comprising about half the entire island have been officially designated as "of outstanding natural beauty" and the National Trust owns tracts of down and shore at the western end.

On the other hand, being seasonal, tourism as the island's main concern creates a need which in the long term might also be seen as a threat to its character and this is the necessity for more manufacturing industry. Many families, resident in the island and of working age, who serve the tourist trade are cast on the dole for six months in the year and will not be content to stay unless alternative employment is available, for their younger members perhaps as full-time career jobs. With deaths exceeding births and many retired people coming to live in the island, more industry is also needed in order to attract younger immigrants and maintain a balanced population. Heavy slumps in shipbuilding and aircraft manufacture in the 1950s have shown that, to provide a steady base, the island industries must also be more diversified. So the County Council now has an Industrial Advisory Panel to watch the present situation and plan for future needs. These can be simply expressed. By the year 2000 the island population might conceivably approach 130,000. Meanwhile, for the next five years population is expected to increase by at least 1,000 immigrants a year, of whom 300 to 400 will be of working age and new housing to accommodate these people has already been approved. To provide jobs for them and to absorb the existing island unemployed (nearly all men) it is calculated that six additional small firms must be started each year, each providing a maximum of one hundred jobs. For this development the necessary land has been earmarked.

One might be alarmed at this prospect if the five years had to be extended to the end of the century, as the tentative population forecast implies, but it must be remembered that immigration can in fact be controlled by the amount and type of house-building approved. At the moment new housing keeps pace with new arrivals, but if this was reduced, immigration would also fall. And, of course, "industry" has a special meaning in the Isle of Wight. Outside the Cowes–Newport area there is no heavy stuff and even here the Council is hoping, much to its credit, to make a Country and Water Park along the banks of the Medina river, masking the uglier buildings and using the old Cowes–Newport railway track as an approach road.

Elsewhere light industry is widely dispersed, never far inland but clustered round the main centres of population. Much of it could more properly be called home crafts. Springs, for instance, are made in the West Wight (in an attractive looking factory on the site of the old Freshwater railway station), but also studio pottery, lampshades and ornamental ironwork. Around Ryde we find chrome plating, electronics, mopeds, fibre-glass hulls; at Bembridge, boat building, hovercraft and aircraft; behind Sandown and Shanklin, confectionery and air conditioning equipment and at Ventnor, souvenir dolls, novelties and plastics. A lot of this activity could never be a threat to the scenery and so far, thanks to careful planning, the larger concerns have been absorbed with barely a tremor. So we must wish every success to the island's industrial schemes. As has been proved, they need not spoil the natural beauty and indeed in one sense they are the essential basis for its preservation. For if the island economy cannot be self-supporting there will be only one alternative, the often reviewed but so far rejected road bridge across the Solent. I need hardly say that such a link would spell death at one blow to the island's peace, seclusion and charm.

Meanwhile, granted a viable economy, including an intensification of horticulture, the island's basic problem remains, in the words of the County Planning Officer, that it is pressed "into the duality of *development* in terms of tourism and recreation and *conservation* of the natural scenic and agricultural heritage". There is ample proof throughout Britain that excessive recreational use of the countryside leads to its ultimate destruction and if this is to be avoided in the island perhaps one day it may be necessary to control the number of summer visitors by restricting the amount of holiday accommodation available. At the present time conservation is being effectively achieved in a number of ways, apart from those already mentioned: by providing ample facilities for conventional summer sports and by encouraging other activities not harmful to the scenery, for instance hiking, through the creation of 135 miles of nature trails mapped and described in County Council leaflets in the same way as the trail at Newtown.

There is one further threat to the character of the island and this comes from the enormous development in the Southampton area under the decentralisation of London scheme. This might well build up great pressure from would-be immigrants which it would be difficult to resist, among them people who crossed for work to the mainland each day, as some of the islanders now do.

In all, then, we cannot be complacent about the future of this beautiful island. We know that in Britain ruthless materialistic civilisation, with all its stupefying horrors, grows with a dynamism almost independent of the human will. From time to time, when on the point of suffocating in its mesh, people escape to the country and rediscover a very basic and powerful need for nature. But with us, unfortunately, nature has almost ceased to be dynamic; we can manipulate and destroy it all too easily, and the necessity not just the desirability of preserving it has only recently begun to percolate our consciousness. Yet the day might well come when some future generation will positively prefer green fields to another shopping precinct, another industrial estate, another atomic power station. We must do our best to ensure that the fields will still be there for the choice to be a real one.

But still, and for many years to come, I sincerely hope, there is plenty of space in the Isle of Wight and no one need be deterred from going by thoughts of the doubled population in summer or the crowded roads. Without building one more bungalow or adding a single chalet to the holiday camps the islanders say that they could provide almost another 300,000 holidays of one week's duration a year *if* more visitors would come near the beginning of the season in May or June or towards the end in September. There is no need, either, if you want a quiet holiday, to be put off by pictures of Sandown beach swarming like an ant-heap. There are five types of holiday provided: yachting (which is increasingly popular), the ant-heap (officially known as "seaside town"), holiday camps (of which there are some finely situated ones on the south coast), camping, or "quiet". The quiet holiday can be found in Totland and the West Wight generally, anywhere along the Undercliff, amongst the inland villages and those nearer to the coast like Brook, Brighstone and Chale.

But for me, the island displays its greatest charm in the off-season, when visitors, one need hardly say, are doubly welcome. More often than not the weather in early October is sunny and with the holiday-makers all gone you can have the downs, the beaches, the roads to yourself. The contrast with mainland congestion is really quite extraordinary. The autumn light filters through reddening leaves on to stone walls and thatch. The village postman cycles past with a half-empty bag. On the whole long shore at Compton there is not a footmark. And the only sounds are the cry of gulls and the steady breathing of the sea. Then it is that you feel that sense of freedom so seldom experienced on the mainland and then, too, you remember the island's coat of arms: a triple castle between three anchors on an azure field supported by a horse and a sea-horse, the shield resting on a green, argent-coasted island lapped by an azure sea, and underneath, the motto: All this beauty is of God.

APPENDIX

CHURCHES

For so small an island there is a large number of churches of great variety and general interest, though they are not particularly memorable from an architectural point of view. They are notable for the amount of well-carved woodwork of late Elizabethan or early seventeenth-century date. Except for traces of Caen stone and Purbeck marble used in pillars, they are built entirely of local stone, either the hard shelly limestone from the north of the island or the less durable, but more easily worked freestone from the Upper Greensand in the south. Many are Norman in origin, but all show considerable later additions or alterations. Saxon churches existed in the island, but almost all trace of them has disappeared.

Arreton. Chancel with south chapel, nave with north and south aisles and west tower. The interior is said to be the most attractive architecturally in the island. Some pre-Norman masonry and a Saxon doorway opening into the belfry. North aisle Norman, chancel and south aisle Early English. Norman, Early English and Tudor windows. In the churchyard are buried Oliver Cromwell's grandson William and Elizabeth Walbridge, heroine of the Rev. Legh Richmond's best-selling story, *The Dairyman's Daughter* (see Brading).

Brading. A dignified, spacious and well-proportioned church, pleasantly situated on high ground at the top of the village where, according to tradition, St. Wilfrid made the first Jutish converts in A.D. 685. Chancel with north and south chapels, a Norman nave of five bays, north and south aisles, western tower with octagonal broached spire. Aisles and tower built about 1250. North and south chapels added in the late fifteenth century. The whole church was carefully restored in

176

1865. On the south side of the sanctuary there is a remarkable and unique fifteenth-century figure in plate armour incised and formerly outlined in silver on a slab of Purbeck marble—John Curwen, 1441, Constable of Porchester Castle. The south Oglander chapel was built in the late fifteenth century. It contains some good effigies and elaborately carved tombs. In the eighteenth century, Rev. Legh Richmond was curate here. His true stories of island life, *The Annals of the Poor*, sold two million copies in the early nineteenth century and were translated into five foreign languages. Another of his heroines, "Little Jane", is buried in the churchyard.

Brighstone. Chancel with south chapel, nave with north and south aisles, west tower with short spire. Original church was built about 1190, but of this only some Norman arches remain. Subsequent, particularly Victorian alterations, when pseudo-features including large windows in the Late Decorated style were added, have completely falsified the original style of the church. Thomas Ken, author of hymns "Glory to Thee, my God, this night" and "Awake, my soul, and with the sun" was rector here, also Samuel, son of William Wilberforce.

Calbourne. One of the oldest churches in the island and very picturesque. There was a church here at the time of the Domesday Survey, but all that remains of it is some masonry in the west wall of the present church which is an expanded and restored version of the Norman original with the addition of a horrifyingly inappropriate side-chapel in the Early English style. In the south aisle are interesting thirteenth-century lancet windows interspersed with masonry. Some good brasses, including one of William Montacute, Earl of Salisbury (died 1397).

Carisbrooke. The most important ecclesiastical building in the island, eleventh century with Early English additions. An impressive tower, about 100 feet high, built in five stages and finished about 1470. But no chancel, the original one having been pulled down in the reign of Elizabeth I as too dilapidated.

Chale. A weather-beaten and somewhat dreary church, partly transitional Norman, but widened and lengthened in the fifteenth century and recklessly restored in Victorian times. A good, plain Perpendicular tower. No trace remains of the original church, consecrated in 1114.

Freshwater. A large, handsome, originally Norman church with transitional work still remaining. Altered in the twelfth and fifteenth centuries; much enlarged and restored in 1874. Lady Tennyson is buried here.

Freshwater Bay. Small and picturesque. One of the few thatched churches in Britain and the only one in the island. Built in 1908 of island stone, mainly for the convenience of visitors.

Gatcombe. Nave, chancel and west tower. Built in the thirteenth century as a private or manorial chapel. Some of the original fabric remains. Some fifteenth-century stained glass representing angels in feathery clothing. Bad Victorian restoration.

Godshill. On top of its hill, where according to legend the foundations were transferred by supernatural forces from their original site in the valley, the church dominates the thatched roofs of one of the island's show-villages. Entirely in fifteenth-century Perpendicular style. The interior is large and bare, with some pretentious monuments.

Mottistone. Chancel with north chapel, nave with aisles, tower with spire. Twelfth century, but ruined by vandalistic restoration in 1863 when the fabric was partly destroyed and used to build a lych gate with fake holy water stoup made of an old domestic mortar and sham churchyard cross.

Newchurch. "New" in the eleventh century when William FitzOsbern ordered a church to be built on this hill-top site to replace a Saxon chapel lower down the valley. Some Norman work remains with additions in successive centuries to accommodate worshippers in this large parish which formerly stretched from Ventnor to Ryde. An excellent fourteenth-century rose window and an attractive weatherboarded tower (mid-eighteenth century). The vestry was once a chantry where masses were said for the soul of one of the four knights, named de Morville, who murdered Thomas à Becket.

Newport. The parish church of St. Thomas à Becket was built in the

1850s to replace a dilapidated older church founded by Richard de Redvers in 1173. The architecture is not remarkable. There is a fine Carolean pulpit with handsome tester dated 1636 and a graceful marble monument commissioned by Queen Victoria to Princess Elizabeth, daughter of Charles I, who died in Carisbrooke Castle.

Niton. Well situated at the foot of St. Catherine's Down. Chancel with south chapel, nave, north and south aisles. In the nave, Transitional Norman arcades. Many changes and additions up to the fifteenth century. A severe restoration in 1864. No trace of pre-Conquest church or its first Norman successor.

St. Lawrence. Walls mainly twelfth century. Until its extension in 1830, the smallest church in England, 25 feet long by 11 feet wide.

Shalfleet. A church has existed here since the eleventh century. Massive tower, 30 feet square, built 1070. Twelfth-century nave, north wall of which was shoddily rebuilt in the nineteenth century. Thirteenth-century chancel and south aisle with fine arcade of Purbeck columns. Unique oval tracery in the south windows. Carolean pulpit.

Shorwell. Originally a chapel for the tenants of Northcourt Manor, built around 1100. Enlarged into a church and then remodelled in the fifteenth century on a curious rectangular plan with three aisles and no separate chancel. Vestry was formerly a chamber for the parish gun. Fourteenth-century stone pulpit. Good Perpendicular windows. Unique wall painting, dated about 1440, over the north door depicting scenes in the life of St. Christopher. Interesting brasses and monuments. In a glass case, a copy of the third edition of Cranmer's Bible.

Whippingham. Designed by the Prince Consort. A peculiar mixture of styles (German lantern tower, rose windows copied from Notre Dame, Gothic arches), but the result is unexpectedly pleasing. The interior, owing to gifts from royalty and others, is more opulent than in other island churches. Fine wrought-iron candelabra, a jewelled Bible, a beautiful reredos of the Last Supper carved in white marble, a fine bronze screen, carpet, stools and prie-dieu worked by Princess Beatrice and ladies of the Court. Prince Louis of Battenberg and

Princess Victoria of Hesse, grandparents of Prince Philip, are buried here.

Yaverland. Built around 1150 as a private chapel to Yaverland Manor. Reconstructed in 1889. Elaborately carved Norman arches and fine alabaster reredos.

Yarmouth. A somewhat gaunt building reconstructed in 1626 from the ruins of an older church, after two previous churches had been destroyed by French raiders. In a side chapel is a marble statue of Sir Robert Holmes, Governor of the island 1668–92, said to have been intended as a statue of Louis XIV and captured with its sculptor from a French ship by Sir Robert who had his own head substituted.

MANOR HOUSES

There are several delightful small manor houses in the island, dating mostly from Elizabethan or Jacobean times, built of the local stone, well preserved, many of them set in charming unspoilt scenery. Some have now been converted into flats or are used as farm-houses. Others are still private homes.

Arreton. Built about 1612 in typical Jacobean style with two projecting wings and a central porch. Now run as a show-place with contemporary furniture, pottery studio, antique shop, toy museum and cream teas in the old kitchen. Fine carved mantelpieces. Well worth visiting.

Billingham House. Georgian, built on three sides of a square on a Jacobean foundation. Plenty of secret panels. A fine staircase attributed to Inigo Jones. Owned at one time by J. B. Priestley who wrote most of his plays here.

Chale Abbey Farm. Traceried windows have wrongly suggested an ecclesiastical connection, hence misnamed "Abbey". A most attractive building with gabled hall and two-storey gabled porch. Dates from the fourteenth century, but much altered since.

Gatcombe. Built in 1750. Almost a square, with three tiers of sash windows. Extremely elegant and well proportioned.

Haseley. Jacobean. A large rambling house with many gabled additions sticking out at odd angles.

Kingston. Small Jacobean, built as a narrow rectangle with fine eighteenth-century brick chimney added.

Merston. Fine Jacobean house of lovely deep red brick. Central porch and unusually projecting wings. Excellent carved oak mantelpieces and panelling in upper rooms.

Mottistone. Most attractive L-shaped building in handsome position with its porch at the junction of the arms. Dates from the early sixteenth century and is built of large blocks of greensand stone. Stone internal door-openings and stone staircase. Square-headed mullioned and transomed windows.

North Court. Near Shorwell. Unconventional two-storeyed Jacobean on an imposing scale with three gables in a row and a fourth projecting at one end. Two sets of bay windows.

Nunwell. The Oglander home set in a fine park under the north slope of Brading Down. Originally Elizabethan, but later additions give the house a typically eighteenth-century appearance, with sash windows and low-pitched roof.

Sheat. Similar to Arreton, but slightly older, in a charming position at the foot of Chillerton Down.

Swainston. Spacious eighteenth-century house at the north foot of the central chalk ridge, burnt out, except for the thirteenth-century hall-cum-oratory, in a 1941 air-raid. Now rebuilt and used as a school.

West Court. On the road from Shorwell to Brighstone. The oldest part dates from Henry VIII. Uneven extensions under Elizabeth I and James I, gables projecting in all directions, massive chimneys and quaint porch make this the most picturesque of island houses.

Wolverton. Small but well-proportioned Jacobean in a secluded position near Shorwell. Stately great hall. Good carved chimney-pieces. One room said to be haunted by the ghost of a murdered musician.

Yaverland. A large house on the usual Jacobean plan, of symmetrical proportions with huge chimneys, beautifully situated on high ground to the east of Sandown Bay. Built by a Welshman who made a fortune selling locally brewed beer to ships victualling at St. Helens.

BIBLIOGRAPHY

At least parts of the following books can be recommended for the information they contain on topics and personalities connected with the island, past or present.

The History, Topography & Antiquities of the Isle of Wight, W. H. Davenport Adams, London, 1856
Englische Charakterbilder, F. Althaus, Berlin, 1869
Poets of the Wight, ed. C. J. Arnell, I.W. County Press, 1922
At War with the Smugglers, F. D. Arnold-Forster, 1936
Further Memorials of the Royal Yacht Squadron, J. B. Atkins, 1939
Nunwell Symphony, C. Aspinall-Oglander, Hogarth Press, 1945
Niton, Isle of Wight, W. H. Bartlett, I.W. County Press, n.d.
Bembridge past and present, E. Du Boulay, 1911
Days in the Isle of Wight, Paul Bourget, London, 1901
The Scandal of Sophie Dawes, Marjorie Bowen, John Lane, 1935
England's Eden, Edmund Burton, Littlebury & Co., n.d.
The Isle of Wight, George Clinch, Methuen, 1904
Yarmouth, Isle of Wight, A. G. Cole, I.W. County Press, 1946
Isle of Wight, its Churches and Religious Houses, J. Charles Cox, Allen & Sons, 1911 (County Churches Series)
Newport in Bygone Days, R. J. Eldridge, I.W. County Press, 1952
Julia Margaret Cameron, her Life and Photographic Work, Helmut Gernsheim, Fountain Press, 1948
Memorials of the Royal Yacht Squadron, Montague Guest and William Boulton, Murray, 1903
Sacred Cowes, A. Heckstall-Smith, Wingate, 1955
The Isle of Wight, Barbara Jones, King Penguin, 1950
The Isle of Wight, R. L. P. and D. M. Jowitt, Batsford, 1951
Dictionary of the Isle of Wight Dialect, W. H. Long, London, 1886
The Oglander Memoirs, ed. W. H. Long, London, 1888
The Queen in the Isle of Wight, A. Patchett Martin, London, 1898

BIBLIOGRAPHY

Fifty Years Back of the Wight, Yarns of Wrecks & Smuggling, F. Mew, I.W. County Press, 1934

The Isle of Wight Bedside Anthology, ed. Hugh Noyes, Arundel Press, 1951

Whippingham to Westminster, Roland Prothero, Murray, 1938

The Pre-Eminent Victorian, A Study of Tennyson, Joanna Richardson, Cape, 1962

The Isle of Wight Railways, Michael Robbins, Oakwood Press, 1953

Isle of Wight, Aubrey de Selincourt, Elek, 1948

Victoria of England, Edith Sitwell, Faber, 1949

The Architectural Antiquities of the Isle of Wight, Percy G. Stone, F.R.I.B.A., 2 vols., London, 1891

Alfred Lord Tennyson, A Memoir, Hallam Tennyson, Macmillan, 1897

Alfred Tennyson, Charles Tennyson, Macmillan, 1950

Queen Victoria's Private Life, E. E. P. Tisdall, Jarrolds, 1961

Isle of Wight, Telford Varley, Cambridge, 1924 (Cambridge County Geographies)

A Guide to the Isle of Wight, Rev. Edmund Venables, London, 1860

The Isle of Wight, J. Redding Ware, London, 1869

The Undercliff of the Isle of Wight, J. L. Whitehead, London, 1911

The Battle of Bonchurch, C. T. Witherby (pub. by the author, Upper Bonchurch), 1962

The History of the Isle of Wight, R. Worsley, London, 1781

British Regional Geology, The Hampshire Basin and Adjoining Areas, 3rd edition, H.M.S.O., 1961

Index